Gustave Courbet

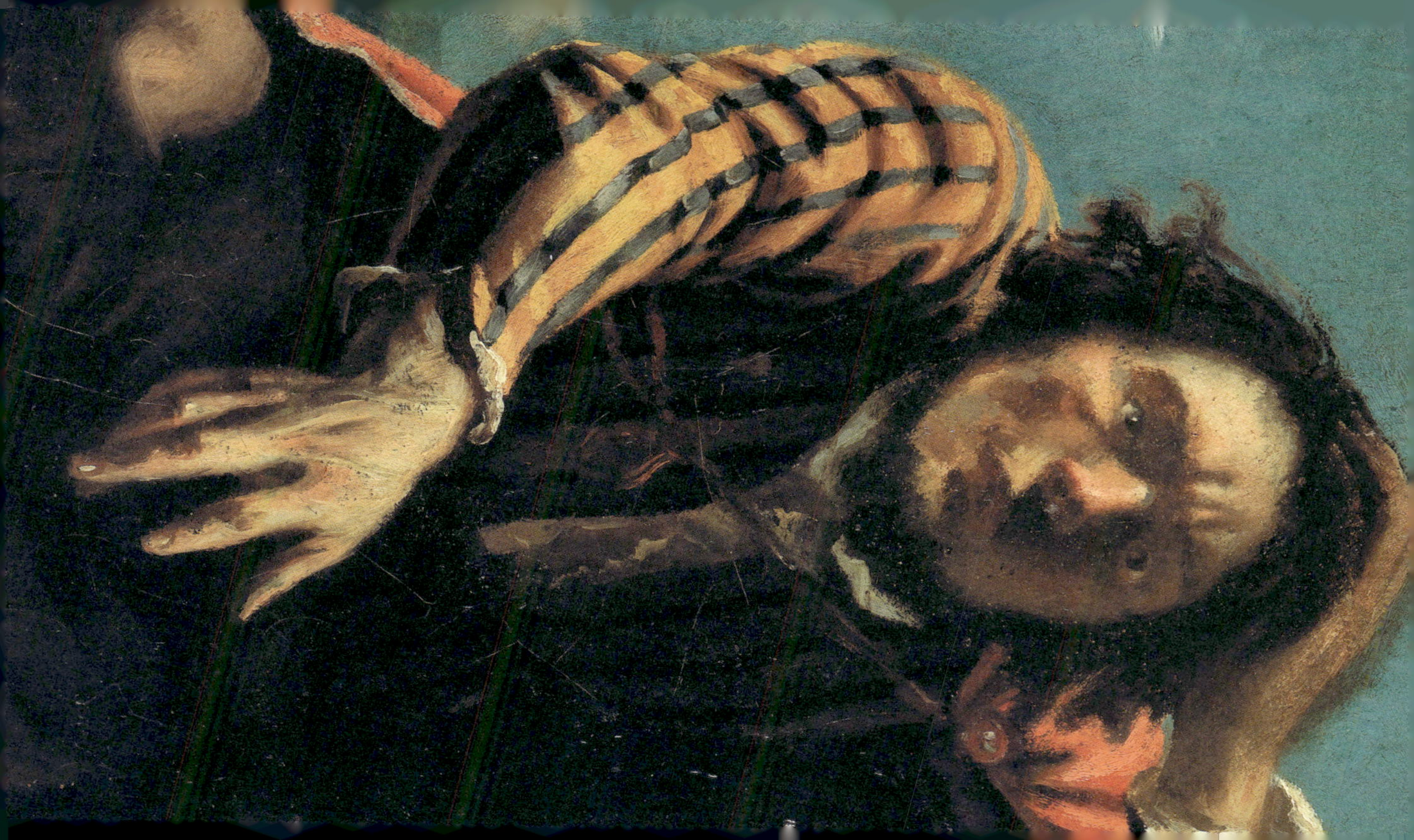

Gustave Courbet

By Ulf Küster

HATJE
CANTZ

Contents

Prologue
The Hammock

I can remember my first encounter with a painting by Gustave Courbet quite vividly. It was in 1971 during a visit to the Oskar Reinhart Collection "Am Römerholz" in Winterthur. I was five years old; my father, as usual, took me by the hand and I know for sure that I was puzzled by the peculiar yellow socks worn by the young girl sleeping in a hammock in Courbet's painting (ill. p. 10/11). Could they be some kind of shoe-socks? Even today, after countless visits to this magnificent museum, I am still puzzled by this odd footwear, which seems better suited to a character in a Biedermeier fairy-tale painting by Ludwig Richter. Her feet are naturally immaculate, as if this beauty never touched the ground before laying herself down to sleep.

Gustave Courbet's *Le hamac (The Hammock)* from 1844 is a masterpiece, a dreamlike vision in every sense of the word. But what does the painting depict? Is it Courbet's dream or the sleeping girl's? One sees a forest clearing; a hammock is stretched over a path that leads in turn to another clearing in the background. A girl lies in it and sleeps, half in sunshine, half in shade. She wears a garland of flowers in her loose blond hair. The weather is apparently very warm because she has removed her blue silk shawl and opened her bodice, lined in yellow, underneath which her breasts are just visible through transparent gauze. The girl's legs hang down from the hammock, feet crossed, her skirt hiked up to reveal calves clad in white stockings. She holds firmly onto the edge of the hammock with her right hand, while her left hand extends over her head in a gesture typical of sleeping persons. Her chin rests on her chest and the expression on her face has something equally lascivious and innocent about it. And in general she seems virginal and a little wicked at the same time. The dream she is presently dreaming is surely very pleasant. It is a pity that it will soon come to an end, because she is about to fall off the hammock. Her hair, which resembles a waterfall, presages her imminent plunge to the ground. She will not fall onto the path itself but rather into shallow, dark water, which will wrench her from her reverie.

This painting often reminds me of two verses from "Frühlingstraum" [Dream of Spring], a poem from Wilhelm Müller's *Winterreise* [Winter Journey] cycle published in 1823 and set to music by Franz Schubert. They concern the abrupt shift from the world of dreams to that of reality, which for Müller was a sign of the difference between the idea of freedom and the reality of suppression during the Restoration and the period leading up to the March Revolution of 1848:

Ich träumte von Lieb' um Liebe,
Von einer schönen Maid,
Von Herzen und von Küssen,
Von Wonne und Seligkeit.

Und als die Hähne krähten,
Da ward mein Herze wach;
Nun sitz' ich hier alleine
Und denke dem Traume nach.

[I dreamt of mutual love,
Of a lovely maiden,
Of embracing and kissing,
Of joy and rapture.

And when the cocks crowed
My heart awoke;
Now I sit here alone
And reflect upon my dream.][1]

Does Courbet's *Hammock* depict the transition from an idealized world to a harsh reality? Is this image of sleep shortly before it comes to an abrupt end also about the end of an era that can be designated "Romantic"? The fact that this painting might unexpectedly contain concealed messages still occupies me today. The garland the young woman wears in her hair is not an ivy wreath, as has frequently been claimed.[2] It is in fact

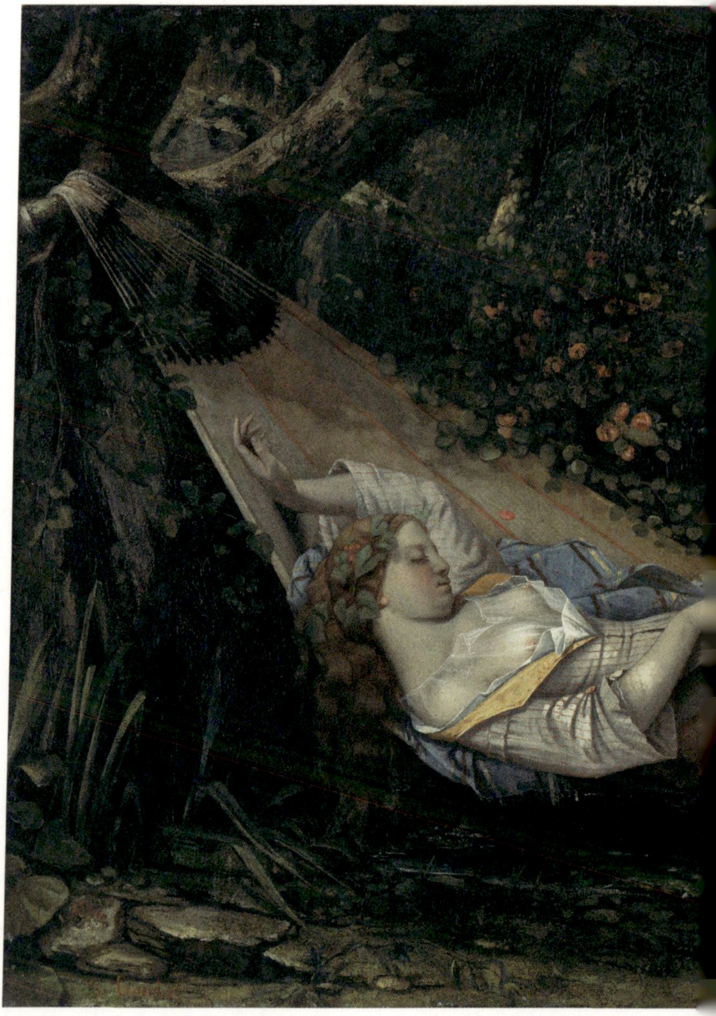

Gustave Courbet, *Le hamac (The Hammock)*, 1844, oil on canvas, 70.5 × 97 cm, Oskar Reinhart Collection "Am Römerholz," Winterthur

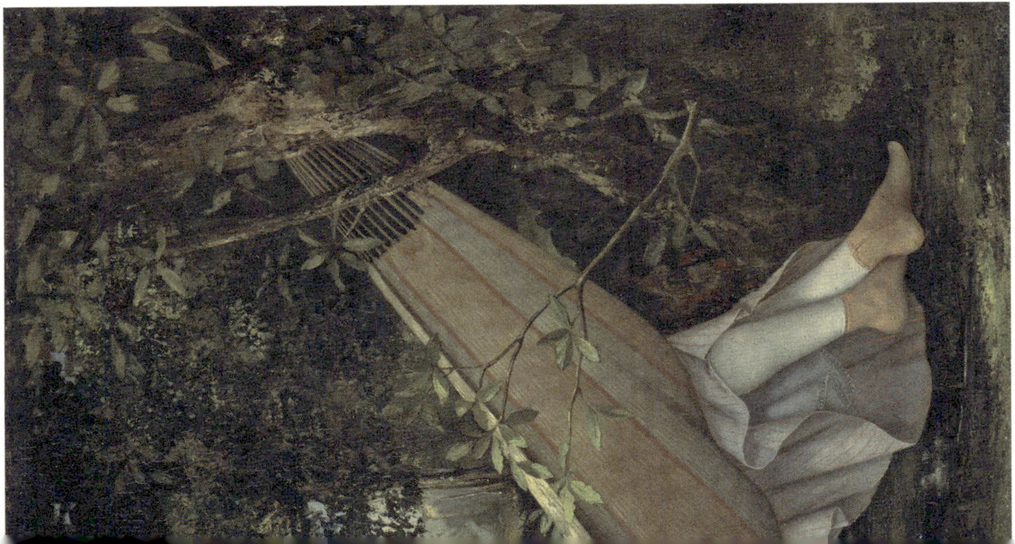

made from black bryony, a medicinal plant with heart-shaped leaves and red berries that, as the French name unmistakably indicates, is traditionally used to treat bruises: "herbe aux femmes battues" (herb of battered women).[3] Other vernacular names include "racine vierge" (maiden root) or "sceau de Notre Dame," which can be translated as "seal of Our Lady." Both names indicate a further function: the plant seems to have been employed as a contraceptive.[4] If Courbet was aware of this, which is likely, then the rude awakening that will follow upon sleep would take on a very different meaning here.

The year before completing this painting, Courbet depicted himself in a self-portrait that was selected in 1844 for the annual public Salon exhibition in Paris—his debut. The *Portrait de l'artiste,* known as *Courbet au chien noir* (*Portrait of the Artist,* known as *Courbet with a Black Dog,* front cover) shows him as a fashionably dressed Romantic wearing plaid trousers, a dapper frock coat, and a hat adorning his magnificently curly head of hair like some murky halo. The artist is seen resting during a walk; he holds a pipe in his hand, while his walking stick and sketchbook lean against the rocks behind him. It appears as if he has given himself over to melancholy, and his glance, looking down his nose at the viewer, seems to underscore the distance between himself and his audience, as if the latter will never be in a position to understand him. And the glance of the dog seated next to the painter also seems to say: "I am the only one who is faithful to you." The background, freely painted—probably with a palette knife—and left unfinished, is conspicuous.

The painting depicts Courbet in the mood he was in when he imagined the women of his dreams in forest clearings, yet not without recalling the unwanted consequences of sexual exuberance.

The Reinhart Collection likewise houses a painting made by Eugène Delacroix in 1844, the same year as Courbet's *Hammock*, namely *La mort d'Ophélie* (*The Death of Ophelia*, ill. p. 14). Delacroix (1798–1863), the most important artist of the Romantic movement in France, was over twenty years Courbet's senior (1819–1877). Here again the painting concerns a young woman and water: in Delacroix's painting, however, she has already fallen into the water, both literally and figuratively. Delacroix's Ophelia is somewhat more buxom compared to Courbet's sleeping girl, and with her completely exposed upper body I always felt her to be much more erotic than the girl on the hammock. As is often the case with Delacroix, his work is a painted elaboration of a scene described in William Shakespeare's tragedy *Hamlet*, though less ambiguous than Courbet's cryptic and much more subtle painting.

But one thing I will never understand is how Ophelia could drown in such a shallow stream; it reminds me of the critical remark Delacroix noted in his journal when Courbet's *Baigneuses* (*Bathers*, Montpellier, Musée Fabre) was exhibited in 1853, stating that the water was a "little puddle scarcely deep enough for a footbath."[5] Courbet may have responded to Delacroix's Ophelia motif, which exists in numerous versions, to the extent that he also painted a picture of a woman bathing

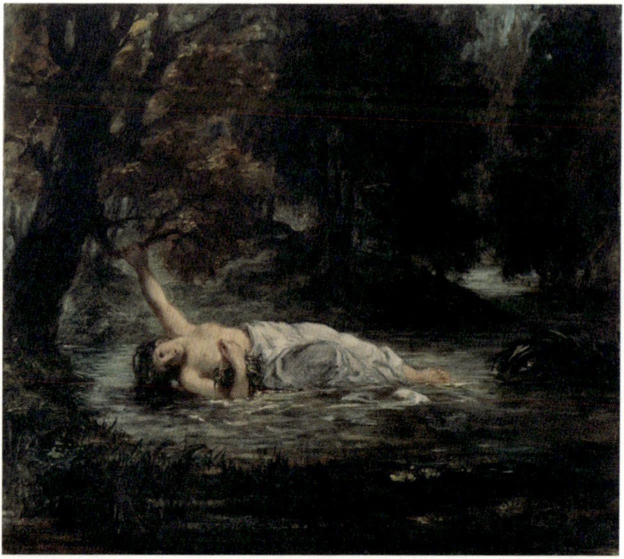

Eugène Delacroix, *La mort d'Ophélie (The Death of Ophelia)*, 1844, oil on canvas, 55 × 64 cm, Oskar Reinhart Collection "Am Römerholz," Winterthur

in a stream in a very similar pose—who, however, is undressed and surely not about to take her own life (Mohamed Mahmoud Khalil Museum, Cairo). Courbet used this motif again in his painting *Trois baigneuses* (*Three Bathers*, 1865–68, ill. p. 15), rotating it by ninety degrees in the process and turning a woman reclining in the water into one who is slipping vertically into the pool. Quite an unusual procedure.[6]

Delacroix and Courbet surely observed each other quite closely. Their—more or less concealed—reactions are a leitmotif in this book, whose seven essays serve as an introduction to

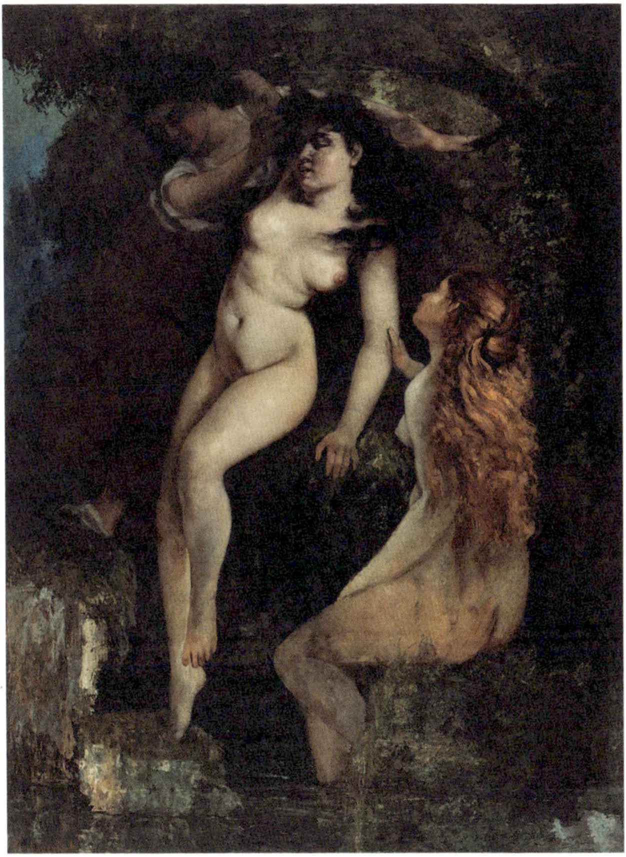

Gustave Courbet, *Trois baigneuses (Three Bathers)*, 1865–68,
oil on paper on canvas, 126 × 96 cm, Petit Palais, Musée des Beaux-Arts
de la Ville de Paris

selected aspects of Gustave Courbet's life and work. It is published on the occasion of the exhibition devoted to Courbet at the Fondation Beyeler. Courbet plays with the expectations of his viewers and the treatment of color; the hidden references to classic art-historical iconography and emphasis on his individuality as an artist make him a seminal figure in the transition from tradition to modernity. He is an artist whose work also fascinates those who are not concerned with art on a daily basis. And perhaps this little book will contribute to the desire to take a fresh look at Courbet and rediscover his immensely rich oeuvre and compelling life.

Ornans – Flagey

May 2013: Underway in Gustave Courbet's native land, in the French part of the Jura. The rain is coming down in sheets—suitable weather for this rural and remote region where water seems to be everywhere. Plateaus alternate with deeply carved valleys through which rivers, springing forth from the depths of the earth in grottos and cascading downward in mighty waterfalls, wind their way. It is as if one is moving about on a giant sponge. This area belongs to Franche-Comté, the "free county," with its capital Besançon, that first became a part of France in 1678; it had previously been under the control of the Habsburgs and the Swiss, and after the mid-sixteenth century even belonged to the Spanish Habsburgs. Its inhabitants are still proud of this Spanish influence; it is considered particularly good form to display a certain independence from Paris. And this was very likely the case in Gustave Courbet's day as well.

He was born on June 10, 1819, officially in Ornans, a bustling town situated twenty-five kilometers from Besançon. The registry at the local town hall does not specifically indicate the place of birth, but notes that his father resided in Flagey near Ornans.[7] Perhaps the story is true, according to which Courbet's mother went into labor while she was on her way from Flagey to her parents' home at Ornans and gave birth to Gustave under an oak tree by the wayside.[8] Although his birthplace has not been definitively determined, Ornans lays claim to him as a renowned native son and he is now omnipresent here. Signs point out the places where he painted his famous pictures. In the heart of town, directly on the banks of the Loue, the little river that flows through the town, stands the house where he was supposedly born along with a museum dedicated to him, which, with considerable support from the regional authorities, has been given a spectacular extension; it also organizes ambitious exhibitions.

Everyone still seems to know everyone else in Ornans, and Courbet is the pride of the community. This was surely also true during the artist's lifetime, despite (or perhaps because of) the fact that—at least according to elderly inhabitants of Ornans, who heard it from their grandparents, who in turn heard it from their grandparents—Courbet often brought scandalous ladies with him from Paris to model for him in his native town. Courbet frequently returned home to Ornans, where he owned property and had a studio in which he painted many of his pictures, often with the active participation of the local populace. One should not underestimate his emotional ties to the region from whence he came. Many of his Parisian friends also hailed from the Franche-Comté or even came from Ornans—for example, his relative, the writer Max Buchon, a childhood friend and classmate. Even during his years of exile in Switzerland, Courbet still produced painted remembrances of his native region, with its high cliffs, watercourses, and orchards through which he had wandered since childhood, and whose grottos he had explored—he is even supposed to have left his name behind in one of them.[9] When a particularly beautiful painting by Courbet came onto the market several years ago—the so-called *Oak at Flagey* from 1864—the residents set up a fund that was ultimately so successful that the town was able to acquire the picture for its local museum.

Courbet's family owned an imposing farm at Flagey, about twelve kilometers from Ornans, which his father brought with him to the marriage. Courbet senior spent most of his time there, while his wife usually lived in Ornans with Gustave and his four younger sisters, probably in her parents' home or in an adjacent building where they resided after the farmhouse at Flagey burnt down in 1827. This stately building, which was subsequently rebuilt, has been recently renovated; exhibitions of contemporary art are now held in the former barn. A café and few guestrooms can be found in the front section of the house today. As a special attraction, I was shown a room with a view of the garden and a comfortable nineteenth-century bed: that this was Courbet's own bed, as I was told, is considered doubtful by the museum at Ornans. The objects in the room that really do derive from the nineteenth century, and perhaps from Courbet's day, are permanently installed pieces of furniture: a kind of desk and a shelf. This alone attests to the fact that Courbet was not a man of the common people by birth. His father not only served as mayor of Flagey for a while, but his property holdings encompassed 168 acres in Ornans and environs, making him the community's largest landowner.[10]

Courbet was very much shaped by his attachment to his native landscape, to the relationship between town and village, between bourgeoisie and peasantry. In Paris he would continue to be seen as the provincial farmer, and if truth be told he actually cultivated this role. But at Ornans he belonged to the upper class. We can say with all due caution that Courbet's family were farmer-townsmen, part of an ancient form of society that lived in urban areas but had considerable land holdings outside city limits. Not only did his father own a farm on the outskirts of the city, but his maternal grandfather Jean Antoine Oudot, a vintner and adherent of the French Revolution, also owned tracts of land outside of the city of Ornans.

The society from which Courbet came was subject to radical structural transformation in the nineteenth century. This is a theme that is also broached in Courbet's paintings. We will illustrate this by means of two seminal realistic works, both of which were exhibited at the 1850 Salon. The first painting, known as *Un enterrement à Ornans* (*A Burial at Ornans,* ill. p. 22/23), was made in 1849/50 on a monumental scale, with a height of 515 cm and a width of 668 cm. The work's full title is "Tableau des figures humaines, historique d'un enterrement à Ornans" (A Painting of Human Figures, the History of a Burial at Ornans). The word "historique" is important; on the one hand it should be understood as a narrative, as a documented story from everyday life.[11] On the other hand, however, it demonstrates Courbet's aspiration to practice the noblest of all artistic genres: history painting.

Influenced by the academies and their associated concepts, art was still shaped by the notion of the hierarchy of genres, which was not only defined by a painting's content, but also by its size. The highest-ranking genre was history painting, followed by portraiture, landscape painting, still lifes, and genre painting. While landscapes, genre scenes, and still lifes were generally small in size, the larger picture formats were reserved for portraiture and especially for history painting.[12] In 1845 Courbet wrote to his parents: "When you don't yet have a reputation you cannot sell easily and all those small paintings do not make a reputation. That is why . . . I must do a large painting that will definitely show what I am really worth. . . . I feel painting should be largely conceived, I want to do large painting."[13]

He realized this objective in *A Burial at Ornans,* and it was surely a courageous enterprise for an artist who never attended a traditional academy. Painted at Ornans, it depicts fifty life-sized figures that, because they all seem to be crowded together in the foreground, have a very immediate impact on the viewer. It goes without saying that the Parisian public was shocked by the direct presence of the figures, particularly as they by no means corresponded to the enraptured idealization one expected when viewing "grande peinture."

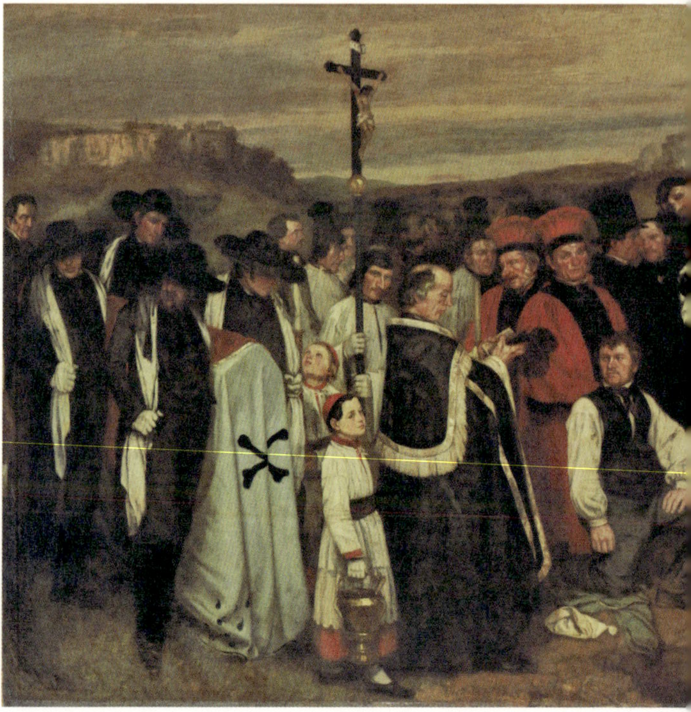

Gustave Courbet, *Un enterrement à Ornans (A Burial at Ornans)*, 1849/50, oil on canvas, 315 × 668 cm, Musée d'Orsay, Paris

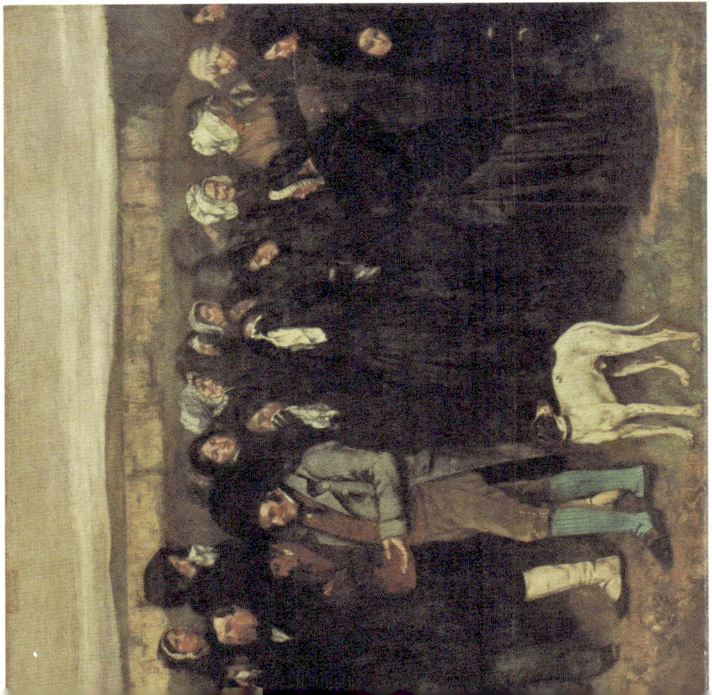

An early photograph which probably dates from the late nineteenth century shows that the group of women standing at the right must have made a much more differentiated impression than is now the case: the varnish applied to the dark clothing in which they are clad has since deteriorated, resulting in greater visual unity than the artist probably had in mind.[14] This makes it even more evident that Courbet did not intend to portray a funeral procession.[15] What we see here is the moment when mourners have arrived at the interment site after having taken the meandering road in the background and gathered around the open grave in the center. They are beginning to form a circle that is also meant to include the viewer, lessening the distance between the viewer and the figures in the painting even further. The priest has taken his position at the graveside along with the crucifix carrier, the choir, the altar boys, and the church officials dressed in their curious robes. Pallbearers are carrying the coffin at the left; the men are standing in the center while the women can be seen at the right. The Parisian audience consequently found itself confronted with a gathering of provincials who, from the perspective of Paris, lived in one of France's most remote regions. As far as the taste of the contemporary public was concerned, Courbet depicted "real" people, people whom he did not idealize or glorify; consequently, they were considered "ugly." Not only can we identify members of his own family, but also the priest of Ornans, the gravedigger, the mayor, and the magistrate, among others. In a letter to his friend Jules Champfleury, Courbet makes fun of the bulbous nose of one of the beadles, saying that it is "as red as a cherry"; he also writes that many people were coming to his studio and specifically requesting to be included in the painting, noting that he might "make quite a few enemies" because he could not immortalize everyone in it.[16]

The site where this scene plays out can still be located today. The occurrence takes place at a cemetery that opened in 1848 on the outskirts of Ornans.[17] But the skull lying alongside the open grave demonstrates that one should not place too much trust in the assumption that Courbet painted an authentic site. It is impossible to find a skull in a cemetery that has only recently been opened. Its depiction here indicates that Courbet was playing with the expectations of experienced contemporary viewers of paintings: skull and gravedigger alongside an open grave recall the famed scene from William Shakespeare's *Hamlet* in which the title character reflects on transience while contemplating the skull of the court jester Yorick. It is more than likely that Courbet's idea of depicting an open grave in the center foreground of his painting was inspired by Eugène Delacroix's 1843 illustration of this scene from *Hamlet.*

But this is not the only quotation in this work. Much about the burial picture is reminiscent of Jacques-Louis David's (1748–1825) monumental 1808 painting *Le sacre (The Consecration),* depicting the coronation of Emperor Napoleon and Empress Josephine in 1804. The priest opening a Bible, for example, looks like a mirror-image paraphrase of Napoleon in David's painting. The figure carrying the crucifix who looks directly at the viewer in Courbet's painting is suggestive of the crucifix carrier in David's picture. The cross similarly seems to hover over the heads of those present, and the staggered arrangement of the figures in Courbet's work likewise calls David's painting to mind.[18]

The painting has no real center in the traditional sense, and this is also unusual for a work that lays claim to being a history painting. The center is the open grave, and the painting's composition is set up in such a way that the viewer must look down into this gaping hole. The two elderly men next to the hunting dog—which has no business being in a cemetery—also direct the viewer's glance to the open grave. The gesture made by the man in the foreground with his left hand is particularly effective in this respect.[19]

But who or what is being buried here? Courbet once claimed that the painting was in reality the burial of Romanticism.[20] Are the Romantic ideals of a very worldly and seemingly illusionless provincial bourgeoisie being laid to rest here? One is reminded of Heinrich Heine's poem from the "Lyric Intermezzo" in his *Book of Songs,* in which the burial of Romanticism is unmistakably described around 1820:

Die alten bösen Lieder
Die Träume schlimm und arg,
Die lasst uns jetzt begraben,
Holt einen großen Sarg.

[The old and evil ballads,
The dreams with bitter sting, —
Come now and let us bury them:
So, a great coffin bring!][21]

Courbet characterized the two men in the right foreground as "Deux vieux de la Révolution de 93," that is to say, "two veterans of the Revolution of 93."[22] Dressed in old-fashioned breeches, gaiters, and tailcoats, the two figures do not really seem to fit in with the group of black-clad mourners. The year 1793, which opened with the execution of Louis XVI, was the most radical year of the French Revolution and the year of the Reign of Terror as well. The old veterans of 1793 are staunch antimonarchists: Does Courbet's painting refer to the then-current political situation? After the February Revolution of 1848, as a result of which the "Citizen King" Louis-Philippe was forced to abdicate the throne, and after the suppression of the workers' uprising in June of that year, the conservative elements of French society that elected Louis-Napoleon Bonaparte, nephew of Napoleon I, as president came to power. The ideals held by the revolutionaries of 1793 resembled those held by the revolutionaries of February 1848, and over the course of the following years until the coup d'état staged by Louis-Napoleon Bonaparte on December 2, 1851, were successively repressed in favor of the monarchy and de facto dictatorship propagated by the president of the republic and future emperor. Is a society laying its democratic ideals to rest here?

Courbet has depicted a gathering of people who were facing great economic and social changes or had already been affected by them. The acceleration of industrialization under the administration of Napoleon III in particular had not been kind to the rural populace. Politically active, Courbet, a friend of the writer and anarchist Pierre-Joseph Proudhon, whom he admired and was influenced by, registered the changes in society unleashed by the political and economic upheavals exactly. His works from this time are documents of the social conditions of the day that were undergoing fundamental changes. As such, the pictures were contemporary history painting as he understood and described it in an open letter to his artist colleagues in 1861: "History painting is essentially contemporary."[23]

Les paysans de Flagey revenant de la foire, Ornans (*The Peasants of Flagey Returning from the Fair, Ornans,* ill. p. 30/31), which was likewise exhibited at the 1850 Salon, depicts from a sociohistorical perspective farmers "aux limites de l'aisance" [at the limits of affluence], meaning that they lived under relatively unstable conditions, susceptible to such disruptive factors as crop failure, which played an important role at the time and triggered an agricultural crisis.[24]

Régis Courbet, the painter's father, is recognizable at the center of the composition. Wearing a peasant smock and a high top hat, he is shown riding his horse, driving home purchases that include two lean head of oxen, which he intends to fatten. Serious und withdrawn, his eyes are focused straight ahead. A younger farmer rides alongside him, gesturing in his direction.

The figure off to the left is probably the ox driver. The riders are followed by two women and a cow, perhaps a dairy cow, that appears somewhat better nourished. One of the two women is carrying a basket on her head. A man with a pannier can be seen behind the women, and a pair of lovers is visible in the background on the right. The foreground is dominated by the depiction of a man smoking a pipe. His clothing seems urban: blue tailcoat, vest, and necktie. He seems to have walked into the picture space from the right. With his right hand he supports a bundle on his back, and in his left hand holds not only an enormous plaid umbrella, but also a leash attached to the hind leg of a pig that he is evidently leading home. He is walking alongside the road on which the other figures are traveling, perhaps so his pig can find something to eat. It is curious that the road on which they travel seems to slope down in front; the spatiality of the painting comes across as highly restricted and has an almost relief-like quality. And the foreground where the man with the pig is located is not convincingly connected to the section of the painting with the central group.

Like *A Burial at Ornans,* this work also caused a scandal in Paris: the public was accustomed to other, more idealized images of country life featuring farmers and peasant women who were better looking and cheerier than Courbet's solemn characters. And if one really wants to depict the hardships of rural life, then one should preferably strike a religiously sentimental, detached tone, as in *The Sower* by Jean-François Millet (1814–1875), which also caused a stir at the 1850 Salon but was received

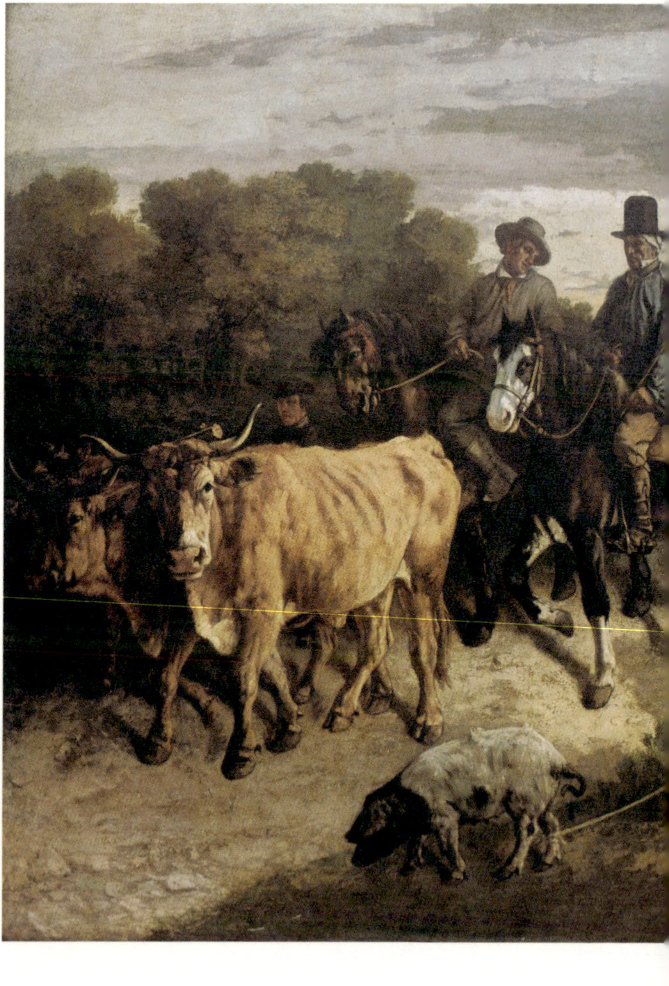

Gustave Courbet, *Les paysans de Flagey revenant de la foire, Ornans (The Peasants of Flagey Returning from the Fair, Ornans)*, 1850, oil on canvas, 206 × 275 cm, Musée des Beaux-Arts et d'Archéologie, Besançon (on permanent loan from the Musée d'Orsay, Paris)

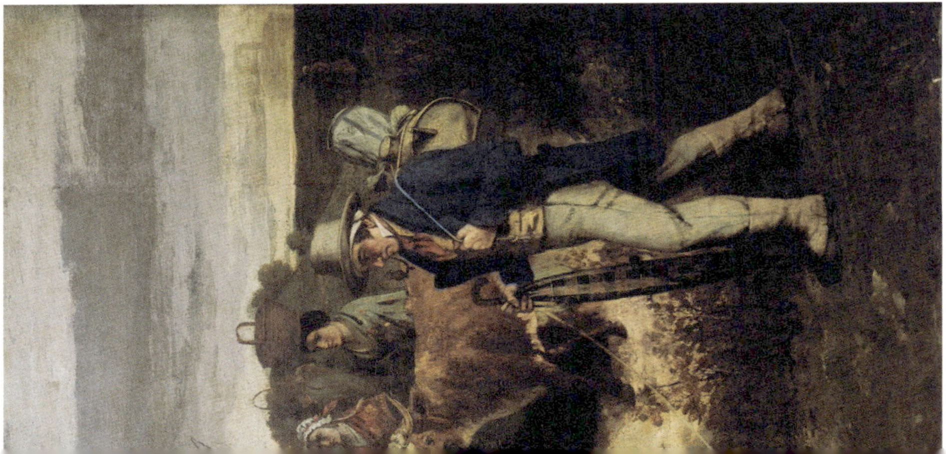

more favorably than Courbet's work. It was considered unseemly that a disheveled pig should be granted so much prominence; the depiction of the characters and their motions was regarded as stiff, which is why caricaturists readily satirized the painting as a gathering of wooden dolls. Even Courbet's manner of painting was rejected: the clayey earth pigments, largely applied with a palette knife, that so wonderfully convey the atmosphere of the Jura were simply dismissed by contemporaries as dirty.

Farmers returning home from market or leading their animals to drinking troughs were above all popular themes in Dutch painting. Courbet, who traveled in the Netherlands in 1846, might have been inspired by works he had seen there.[25] Perhaps Courbet's farmers on their way home represent something like a satire on the theme of the triumphal march that was so very popular in the art of the Late Renaissance and the Baroque. He could also have seen such works in the Netherlands—for example, a detail from the relief *The Triumphal Procession of Fabius Maximus,* executed by Artus Quellinus the Elder (1609–1668) in 1655 for Amsterdam's town hall, shows two horsemen, one of whom turns to the other, as in Courbet's picture.[26]

This is an important motif: it is somehow like a question posed to the father in the painting, a moment of pause and examination that constructs a certain tension between the two characters and emphasizes the figure of the father. The solemnity of the rural triumphal march, in which the newest acquisitions from market are driven home like spoils of war, is interrupted by the peculiar pig-driver in the foreground. Courbet's father and his companion do not wear tailcoats, but they are on horseback and as such are privileged; the foppishly dressed man with the pig, by contrast, is on foot. It is unusual for a farmer to have an umbrella with him and to return home from market dressed in a frock coat. Could he be a city dweller who is acting as if he were a farmer?

The ideal of life in the country, which played a significant role in Paris at the time, was a theme often dealt with by caricaturists, especially Honoré Daumier (1808–1879).[27] The relationship between town and country was marked by great tension, whereby "town" by no means refers only to "Paris." The example of the Courbet family, who were rural landowners on the one hand but also small-town residents on the other, makes this field of tension particularly evident. Investments made by the bourgeoisie in the countryside caused traditional agriculture-oriented society to become dependent. Added to this were several extremely cold winters in the years prior to 1850—Courbet mentions them in his letters—that resulted in considerable crop failures and ultimately an agricultural crisis. And all of this played itself out against the backdrop of a general agro-technical revolution in which, as we shall see, Courbet's father participated. The development that also led farmers to protest Louis-Napoleon Bonaparte's coup d'état of 1851 was in no way limited to the Franche-Comté and was closely observed throughout the country. The prefect of the Departement Drôme even spoke of a "war between the peasant's smock and the suit" in a report dating from December 1849.[28] Courbet, who could not have known this remark, seems to have dealt with this very conflict in his painting of farmers on their way home.

Industrialization in the Countryside
Remarks on *The Stonebreakers* and *The Wheat Sifters*

Among the sheer inexhaustible holdings of the library at the National Gallery of Art in Washington DC, the so-called "vertical files" contain a New Year's card sent by the E. A. Seemann publishing company in Leipzig with best wishes for the coming year of 1959. The greetings sent by publishers that had been nationalized several years earlier featured a poem by Johannes R. Becher, the recently deceased former East German minister of culture, and a reproduction of Gustave Courbet's 1849 painting *Les casseurs des pierres* (*The Stonebreakers*, ill. p. 36). On the reverse it is noted that the original painting fell victim to the flames of the "Anglo-American terror attack on Dresden" on the night of February 13, 1945.

It appears that the painting, which measured 165 × 257 cm, was one of 154 works loaded on a truck and ready for evacuation, but had yet to leave the city on the night in question. The painting has been missing ever since. It had been acquired for Dresden's art collections by its director, Woldemar von Seidlitz, in 1904 and one could almost say that it is an irony of history that this of all paintings was among the losses suffered by Dresden's museums. Had it survived, it could have played a significant ideological role in the former German Democratic Republic,

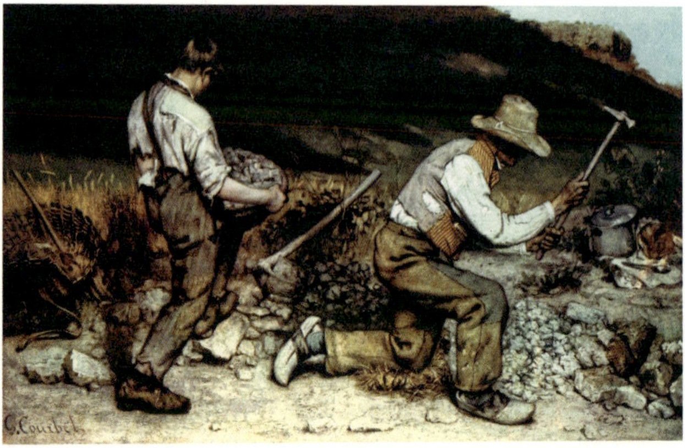

Gustave Courbet, *Les casseurs des pierres (The Stonebreakers)*, 1849, oil on canvas, 165 × 257 cm, formerly Galerie Neue Meister, Dresden (probably destroyed in 1945)

but in the end it was perhaps more valuable to the East German regime as a lost masterpiece of realism than as an existing painting.

In any case, soon after its completion Courbet's painting had become an icon of realism and a powerful indictment of the social condition of the working class. It is not clear, however, whether Courbet initially planned the painting to protest social inequality or whether he simply found the motif of the two stonebreakers to have a particular painterly quality. The painter and writer Alexandre Schanne, a member of the bohemian circle in the Quartier Latin that included Courbet and Pierre-Joseph Proudhon, who was memorialized as the painter

Schaunard in Henri Murger's novel *Scènes de la vie de bohème,* records in his *Souvenirs de Schaunard* a conversation he overhead between Courbet and Proudhon, in which the latter asked:

> "Tell me now, Citizen Master Painter, what brought you to do your stonebreakers?" Courbet is supposed to have simply replied: "I found the motif picturesque and suitable for me." "What? Nothing more?" replied Proudhon. "I cannot accept that such a subject be treated without a preconceived idea. Perhaps you thought of the sufferings of the people in representing two members of the great family of manual laborers exercising a profession so difficult and so poorly remunerated?" "You are right, Citizen Philosopher, I must have thought of that." And from that time on it was not unusual to hear Courbet say: "One would think I paint for the pleasure of it, and without ever having meditated on my subject. . . . Wrong, my friends! There is always in my painting a humanistic philosophical idea more or less hidden. . . . It is up to you to find it."[29]

Alexandre Schanne's recollections, which also include a number of other interesting anecdotes about Courbet, were published in 1887, ten years after Courbet's death and long after the above conversation took place: one should naturally take its contents with a grain of salt. And yet the cited passage demonstrates in exemplary fashion how the wishful thinking that attaches itself to works of art does not necessarily correspond to the artist's original intentions, which may have been merely shaped by formal or aesthetic considerations. Similar remarks made by Courbet have been recorded elsewhere—for example, that he unwittingly addressed himself to social issues in a broader sense in his paintings, when in fact he only intended to point to a particular injustice.[30] He furthermore points out in his famous *Manifeste du Réalisme* of 1855 that the designation "realist" was forced upon him.

In the case of *The Stonebreakers*, we are well informed about the painting's genesis thanks to a letter Courbet wrote to his friends Marie and Francis Wey on November 26, 1849:

> I had taken our carriage to go to the Castle of St. Denis to paint a landscape. Near Maizières I stopped to contemplate two men who were breaking stones on the road. It is not often that one encounters the most complete image of poverty, and so, right then and there, I got the idea for a painting. I told them to come to my studio the next morning and between then and now I have painted my picture. . . . On one side is an old man of seventy, bent over his work, his sledgehammer raised; his skin is burned by the sun, his face is shaded by a straw hat. His pants, of a coarse material, are patched everywhere, and inside his patched clogs his heels show through socks that were once blue. On the other side a young man with dusty hair and a swarthy complexion. His filthy and tattered shirt reveals his sides and arms. A leather suspender holds up what is left of his trou-

> sers, and his muddy leather shoes show gaping holes on every side. The old man is kneeling, the young man is standing behind him energetically carrying a basket of broken stones. Alas, in that class that is how one begins and that is how one ends up. Scattered here and there is their gear, a hod, a hand barrow, a hoe, a farmer's cooking pot, etc. All of this takes place in bright sunshine, in the middle of the countryside beside a ditch next to the road. The landscape fills the canvas. Yes . . . we must drag art down from its pedestal. . . . For too long painters, and even my contemporaries have based their art on ideas and stereotypes.[31]

First of all, Courbet's letter contains what is perhaps the most sensitive description of this painting imaginable. It is interesting to observe that he apparently had no problem in noting that he was traveling about in a carriage when he encountered the two workers, taking the class difference between himself and the stonebreakers for granted. The fact that they caught Courbet's eye at all, the fact that they were working on this very street at all, might have something to do with the renovation of France's road network in the wake of industrialization. During the first half of the nineteenth century, the so-called macadam type of road construction, a forerunner of modern tar surfacing, was introduced in Europe. It was developed in the early nineteenth century by the Scottish engineer John Loudon McAdam, from whose name the designation derives. The method involved layering the road's substructure with stones of different sizes, which, before the introduction of rubble crunching machinery, had to be done by hand.

The work was often assumed by former farmers who were freed by the French Revolution but whose farms were too small and consequently had to be given up as a result of agrarian reforms, or who lost the right to pasture their cattle on fallow land and stubble fields if they themselves did not own any land. Throughout Europe, an attempt was made at that time to consolidate fields, and the stones needed for road building were mostly gathered in the fields. Could it be that Courbet's father also profited from this so-called land enclosure reform?[32] Is it possible that people like the stonebreakers depicted here were dependent on the landowning class, to which Courbet's family belonged?[33]

In a letter written to Champfleury in February or March 1850, in which, significantly, he characterizes the old stone breaker as a "vieille machine," an old machine, Courbet describes the visitors to his studio, the wine growers and farmers, all of whom said that even if he had painted 100 more pictures, none of them could be truer than this one.[34] And Proudhon is reputed as saying that the farmers wanted to purchase *The Stonebreakers* in order to place it on the altar of the church at Ornans.[35]

What "realism" means with regard to Courbet is exceptionally evident here: although the painting is generally regarded as particularly "true to life," the artist was very meticulous in composing it: the two workers posed for Courbet in his studio, and the painting's composition is clearly structured and by no means unconventional. The viewer again recalls classic influences: a depiction of the Adoration of the Magi could have served as the model here. The use of a generally familiar pictorial formula led to the theme's stylization, making exaltation of the painting possible to such an extent that even using it as an altarpiece was taken into consideration.

Courbet's painting *Les cribleuses de blé* (*The Wheat Sifters*, ill. p. 44/45), which was exhibited at the 1855 Salon, likewise depicts a typical rural occupation—namely, two women and a boy separating the wheat from the chaff before milling. The painting, which measures 131 × 167 cm, is not only much smaller than *The Stonebreakers* but also makes a very different impression, at least far as we can judge, given that the earlier painting has been lost. Courbet's *Wheat Sifters* appears much brighter; never before and never again did Courbet employ such a bright palette. Particularly conspicuous is the thickly applied paint, the red of the dress worn by the figure in the middle, and the basic ochre tone of the painting as a whole, which recalls the color of grain: it is as if the choice of colors was inspired by Camille Corot (1796–1875).

According to an old tradition, Courbet's sister Juliette is depicted at the left while the woman in the middle, whose face is turned away from the viewer, is supposed to be the artist's sister Zoë. The assumption that the women here are the painter's sisters apparently refers to a subtitle employed when the painting was shown at an exhibition in Besançon in 1860: "Les enfants des cultivateurs du Doubs"—namely, "The Children of the Farmers from Doubs," which of course is not compelling evidence that the women seen in this work were Courbet's sisters. The hypothesis that the boy at the right is either a portrait of Courbet's illegitimate son Désiré Binet or even a self-portrait of the artist as a child is equally unprovable.[36]

Sifting or winnowing wheat was a complicated and tedious task that could occupy a whole family, even one that lived on such a stately farm as the Courbets' at Flagey, where they surely employed several maids and farmhands. It began after the threshing, i.e. separating the edible grain from the ears of wheat, leaving behind small amounts of straw, chaff, kernels, and weeds—a great many of which were also harvested along with the grain in the days before effective fertilizer. The young woman at the left is probably carrying out a kind presorting, picking out the coarsest pieces of straw and throwing them onto the floor, which is already completely covered with refuse. The presorted grain has apparently been collected in the bowl in the right foreground. The woman in the middle sifts this presorted grain so that the kernels and all other larger elements remain in the sieve while the hull and smaller seeds fall to the ground. This is a strenuous task and explains the position assumed by the woman: the sieve must be moved back and forth with some momentum, meaning that one must kneel on the ground with legs apart in order to support the body and not to fall over. The refuse falls onto a sheet that has been spread out on the ground and will then be removed after the chore is finished, easing the task of cleaning the room afterwards.

The device at the right operated by the seated boy is a winnowing machine, also known as a winnowing fan. Winnowing, which was apparently invented in China, was common throughout Europe by the eighteenth century. By turning a crank on the reverse of the machine shown here, the mixture of straw, hull, and seeds of both weeds and wheat are made to swirl about; by taking advantage of their different weights, it was possible to direct the diverse elements into different conduits. This can be seen at the lower right: the machine has two openings; kernels fall from the one on the right into a bowl, while refuse falls onto the white sheet from the opening on the left.[37]

It is uncertain whether the winnowing fan is depicted in the painting to illustrate the work process or whether Courbet included here because in the future it would make the task carried out by the women superfluous.[38] At the time Courbet painted the picture, an innovative winnowing fan was introduced in Europe, the so-called "Trieure" manufactured by a miller named Vachon in Lyon in 1845.[39] It was presented at the 1851 Crystal Palace Exhibition in London and created a stir in Paris at the 1855 Exposition Universelle. It is not certain whether such a device is the one seen in Courbet's painting. We do know, however, that Courbet's father was interested in the improvement of agricultural machines: he constructed an innovative chain harrow, even publishing his invention in the local newspaper, as mentioned by his son in a letter.[40] The Courbet family was obviously interested in agricultural reforms.

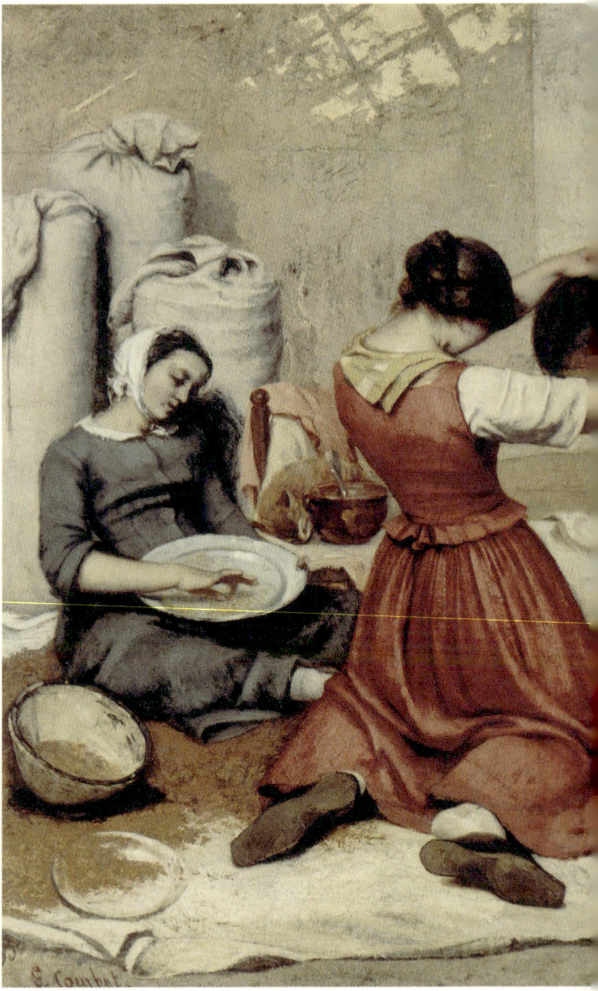

Gustave Courbet, *Les cribleuses de blé (The Wheat Sifters)*, 1853/54, oil on canvas, 131 × 167 cm, Musée des Beaux-Arts, Nantes

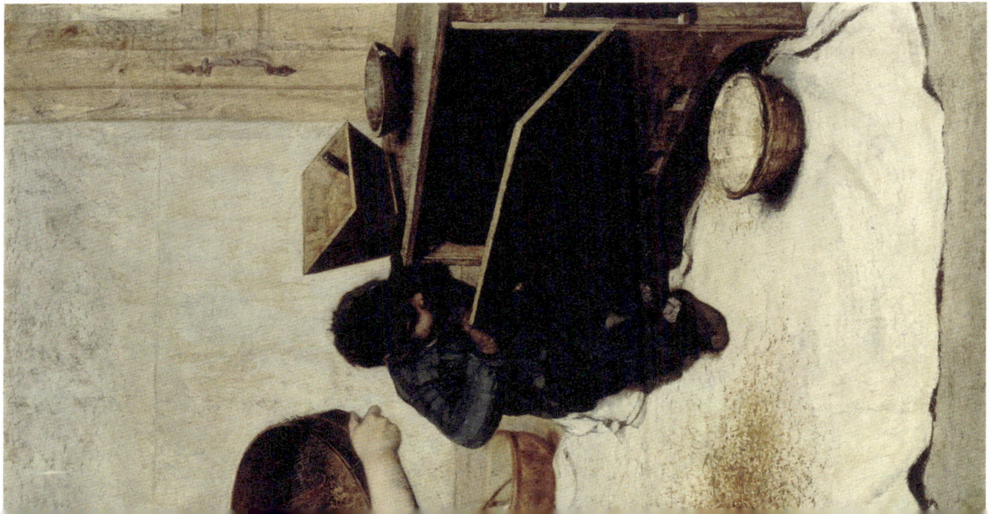

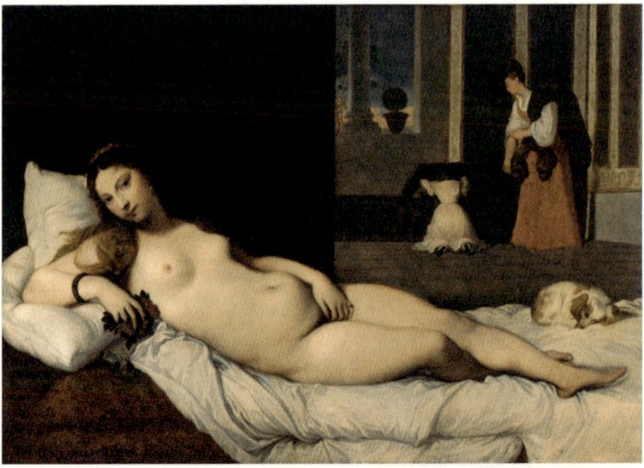

Jean-Auguste-Dominique Ingres, *La Venus d'Urbino (Venus of Urbino)*, copy after Titian, 1822, oil on canvas, 116 × 168 cm, The Walters Art Museum, Baltimore

And what about the inquisitive young boy who operates the machine, opening up the box on the side into order to take a look inside the device? By doing so he would actually be interrupting the work process, and in fact whirling grain should now be flying out of the machine. But Courbet does not depict this. Consequently, his painting is not a faithful documentation of an operational procedure. One cannot see anything in the interior of the apparatus; instead one looks into impenetrable darkness of a type often encountered in Courbet's paintings—the gaping hole of the grave from the large burial painting, or the dark zones in pictures of grottos and waterfalls, which will be discussed in chapter 4. And the motif of a curious child is one that Courbet would take up again.

In his account of the 1855 Salon, Edmond About, who liked the painting in general, found the unconventional position of the kneeling woman's legs to be "more than trivial; she is nearly indecent."[41] It was simply not done for a woman to spread her legs in this manner or let herself be portrayed in this pose. Nor was this motif the only one that led to an eroticized interpretation of the picture: the shower of grain residue falling from the sifter recalls the golden rain Zeus adopted as a disguise when he seduced Danaë.[42]

Courbet was not the first to paint a kneeling woman seen from behind, and here too he appears to be referencing a famous work of art from the past—namely, Titian's 1538 painting of the *Venus of Urbino,* which is regarded as one of art history's great erotic masterpieces (see Ingres' copy, ill. p. 46). In the right background of this painting we see a woman wearing a red dress and a white blouse with rolled up sleeves. She is holding open the lid of a chest, before which another woman kneels and reaches inside. The viewer cannot see what she is doing there or what is inside the chest.

Courbet did not copy this scene, but he did paraphrase it in his painting of the wheat sifters. Perhaps one should not go so far as to suggest that the ostensible passivity of the seated woman at the left of his painting should be linked to the reclining Venus. But Courbet had only to shift Titian's figure of the kneeling woman slightly for his own depiction. There is also every indication that the dress of the sifting woman was inspired by the dress of the standing woman in Titian's painting. And the motif of the opened box, the inside of which remains invisible to the viewer, could likewise have been borrowed from Titian's picture. The line of the edge of the chest lid slanting to the left plays an important role in the composition of Titian's painting because, if extended, it leads directly to the lap of Venus; this compositional idea is similarly taken up by Courbet: the edge of the opened lid of the device, whose brightness makes the darkness of the interior appear ever more intense, places an important accent in the composition of his painting by pointing to the figure in the center. Even the motif of the sleeping dog shows up in Courbet's work lying between the two women.

How did Courbet become familiar with Titian's painting? He never visited the Uffizi in Florence, where the original hangs. Could he have known an engraved reproduction, or the copy painted by his colleague Jean-Auguste-Dominique Ingres (1780–1867), now in the Walters Art Museum in Baltimore (ill. p. 46)? The latter is a possibility; at least, it is possible to place this painting in Paris, where in 1867 it entered the famed collection of Khalil Bey, who also owned pictures by Courbet.[43]

Eugène Delacroix Sees *The Painter's Studio*

On August 3, 1855, the fifty-seven-year-old Eugène Delacroix visited the Exposition Universelle in Paris. The exhibition's international fine arts section, which included artists from twenty-eight nations, also featured a special presentation dedicated to his work and that of his artist colleagues Jean-Auguste-Dominique Ingres, Horace Vernet, and Alexandre-Gabriel Decamps. On the day in question, however, Delacroix visited the section devoted to machines, where he "noticed the fountain that sprouts artificial flowers," among other things. The artist was troubled by all of this: "I think all these machines are very depressing. I hate these contrivances that look as though they are producing remarkable effects entirely on their own volition."[44] Put in a skeptical mood by these devices—an attitude that appears very modern to us today—he decided to go and see the Courbet exhibition that was on show immediately adjacent to the Exposition.

The thirty-six-year-old Gustave Courbet had been angered by the rejection of three of the paintings he submitted to the jury responsible for the art section—although, truth be told, eleven of his pictures had in fact been accepted. He might also have been angry that he and his paintings were not given the same treatment that had been granted others—for example, Delacroix. In any case, it was not without strategic calculation that he put together an exhibition of his own works, showing them in a temporary pavilion he had erected especially for this purpose next door to the Exposition venue. A sign placed over the door read: "DU REALISME. G. Courbet. Exposition de quarante tableaux de ses œuvres" (ON REALISM. G. Courbet: Exhibition of forty of his paintings). Organizing a separate exhibition to show exclusively his own paintings was not the only extraordinary thing about this endeavor—he also charged admission. Courbet had become an "exhibition artist," one who not only painted to sell his pictures but also put them on show at a price.[45] He had already done so previously in the French provinces and Germany as well—with varying degrees of success. But while Courbet's pavilion caused quite a sensation in the artistic circles of Paris, the critics wrote mostly about the pictures that were on show in the "official" Exposition. In the end, his elaborate plan was not worthwhile financially. Delacroix noted in his journal that Courbet had lowered the admission fee and that he himself had spent almost a whole hour there "alone."

> After leaving (the International Exposition in Paris), I went to see Courbet's exhibition; he has reduced the admission to ten cents. I stay there alone for nearly an hour and discovered a masterpiece in the picture they rejected; I simply could not tear myself away from the sight of it. He has made

> tremendous progress, and yet it made me admire his *Burial at Ornans.* ... In this picture the figures are all on top of one another and the composition is not well arranged, but some of the details are superb, for instance, the priests, the choir-boys, the weeping women, the vessel for Holy Water, the women who have broken down in tears etc. In *(The Studio)* the planes are well understood, there is atmosphere, and in some passages the execution is really remarkable, especially the thighs and the hips of the nude model and the breasts, the woman in the right foreground wearing a shawl. The only fault is that the picture, as he has painted it, seems to contain an ambiguity. It looks as though there were a real sky in the middle of the painting. They have rejected one of the most remarkable works of our time, but Courbet is not the man to be discouraged by a little thing like that.

Delacroix wrote about the two principal works in Courbet's pavilion because of their sheer monumental size alone: *A Burial at Ornans* (see p. 20ff) from 1849 and *L'atelier du peintre (The Painter's Studio,* ill. p. 54/55) from 1855, which measures 361 × 598 cm. Briefly summarized, Courbet's painting of his studio shows himself in center of the composition painting a landscape that can be seen on the easel. An undraped woman stands behind him, watching the artist at work. She holds a sheet before her body; her clothing lies on a stool and on the floor. A young boy likewise observes both painter and picture, while a white

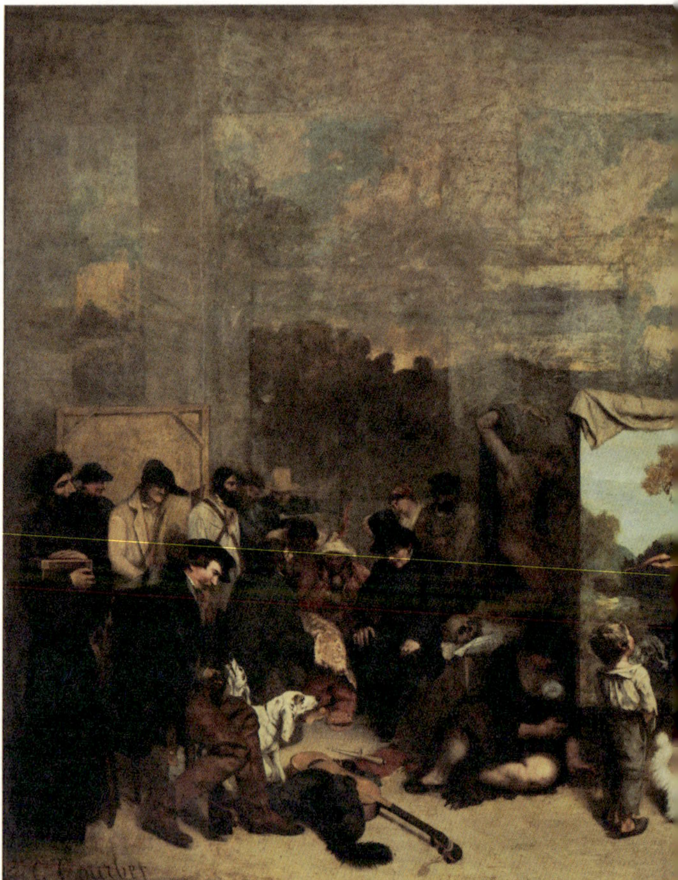

Gustave Courbet, *L'atelier du peintre, allégorie réelle déterminant une phase de sept années de ma vie artistique (et morale) (The Painter's Studio: A Real Allegory of a Seven Year Phase in my Artistic and [Moral] Life)*, 1855, oil on canvas, 361 × 598 cm, Musée d'Orsay, Paris

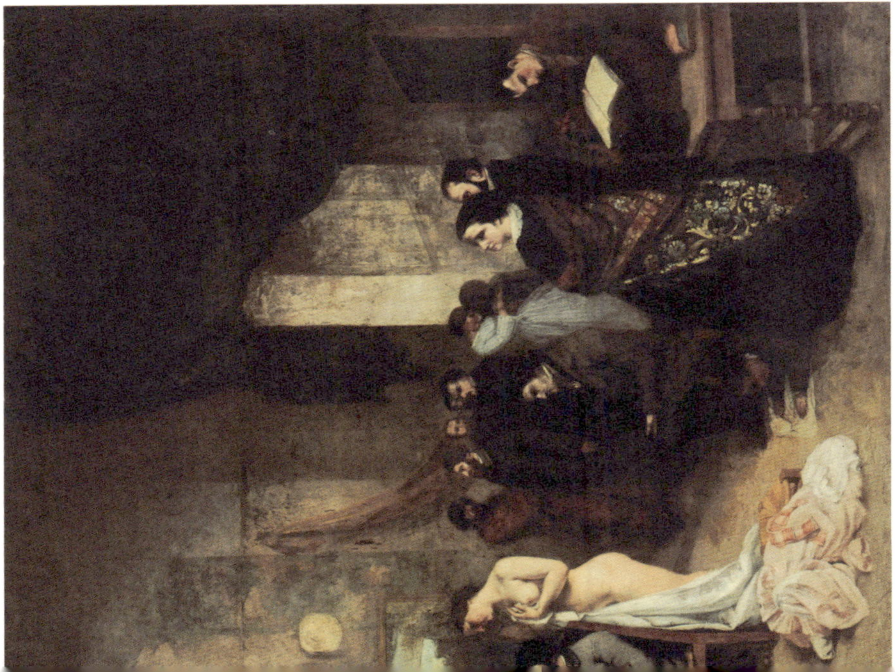

cat plays on the floor between him and model. As we learn from a letter addressed to Champfleury,[46] the group at the left consists of various representatives of the common people to whom the painter felt especially attached. To the right of Courbet, one sees a gathering of his friends and acquaintances. Like the representatives of the common people, they appear as witnesses and guarantors of the painter's work. The entire scene takes place in a large room where paintings are hanging on the walls.

Delacroix's remarks about his colleague are remarkably commendatory. Separated in age by twenty years, the older Delacroix's father was a member of the national assembly during the French Revolution and served for a time as minister of foreign affairs, while the younger Courbet came from a rural, provincial bourgeois background. He furthermore emerged on the scene with the intention of doing much in opposition to traditions that Delacroix held dear, despite the latter's being an artistic innovator himself. Delacroix judges Courbet's work from the perspective of an artist who knows what it is like to stand before an empty canvas and compose a monumental painting. It is something extraordinarily difficult, particularly when a three-dimensional scene is to be translated to the two-dimensional picture plane. Delacroix's criticism of Courbet's first monumental painting, *A Burial,* should be seen against this backdrop. The distribution of mass and the staggered arrangement of the figure groups seem less successful here than his composition for *The Artist's Studio.* Delacroix could not accept the possibility that the crowding of the figures in *A Burial* might have been intended. His own authoritative notion of art was one that developed in the direction of a classic illusionistic ideal and—perhaps—he surmised that it was precisely this approach that was being called into question in the studio painting, which in his eyes was the more successful of the two pictures. We will return to this matter shortly.

It is similarly evident that—as opposed to the countless interpretations this painting has inspired to the present day—Delacroix says hardly a word about what it depicts, about its contents, or even about its possible meaning.[47]

Nor does Delacroix cite the work's complete title, which is: "L'atelier du peintre, allégorie réelle déterminant une phase de sept années de ma vie artistique (et morale)," or: "The Painter's Studio: A Real Allegory of a Seven Year Phase in my Artistic and (Moral) Life." Delacroix does not seem to be have been bothered by the contradiction inherent in the designation "allégorie réelle" (can an allegory be "real"?) because he himself had in fact already painted the ultimate "Allégorie réelle" a quarter of a century earlier, albeit without designating it as such: *Liberty Leading the People*, his painting commemorating the July Revolution of 1830, in which we see the revolutionaries being led by a half-naked woman holding the Tricolore, about whom Heinrich Heine states that she "nearly" resembles "an allegorical figure," likening her to a "Venus of the alleyways."[48] Was Courbet perhaps thinking of Delacroix's *Liberty* when he chose the title or painted the principal female character in his *Studio*? In any case, his female nude makes quite a worldly impression to the extent that she has just removed her everyday clothing. However, she modestly holds a sheet before her body, which in turn is reminiscent of the *Venus pudica* (modest Venus), one of the types of Venus known from classical sculpture. In this sense, and in Heine's eyes, she could be something like a "modest Venus of the alleyways."

But what is the painting's true subject? That is a question for which there is no—and can never be any—simple answer. Courbet says as much in a letter addressed to a friend: "Perhaps you would like to know the subject of my picture; it will take so long to explain that I want to let you guess when you see it. It is the story of my atelier, what goes on there morally and physically. It is fairly mysterious, and will keep people guessing!"[49]

Courbet painted the picture in his studio at Ornans. However, the atelier we are concerned with here is the one in Paris on the Rue Hautefeuille, so it is impossible to tell whether the space has been faithfully rendered. This and further information can be gleaned from Courbet's above-mentioned letter to his friend Champfleury dating from November or December 1854, in which he explains the layout of the work he had just begun and also provides some details about his momentary melancholy—his depression, in fact: "I am in a sad state of mind, my soul drained, my heart and spirit filled with bitterness."[50]

This letter should be treated with caution: while the description of the painting agrees in broad strokes with the completed results, Courbet made some crucial changes that deviate from what he wrote to Champfleury. The sequence of the figures at the left as set out in the letter differs from the completed work, and several of the persons mentioned as being on the right were not depicted in the end. But most of the changes made by Courbet were in the painting's central scene. According to the letter to Champfleury, the artist had initially intended on depicting a satirical scene here. That fact that Courbet ultimately decided on showing a landscape painting on the imagined easel contributed much to the painting's mysteriousness, but also heightened its artistic message.

The only criticism of the *The Artist's Studio* expressed by Delacroix refers to a detail in the central group. The original journal entry states: "La seule faute est que le tableau qu'il peint fait amphibologie: il a l'air d'un vrai ciel au milieu du tableau."[51] This passage is usually translated as "The only fault is that the picture, as he has painted it, seems to contain an ambiguity. It looks as though there were a real sky in the middle of the painting." Delacroix employs the word "amphibologie," the English equivalent of which is "amphibology," a term deriving from logic and linguistics describing a statement whose structure leads it to have more than one meaning.

What induced Delacroix to employ a term such as "amphibologie," which is extremely rare in art theory? Perhaps he was familiar with César Dumarsais's definition in Diderot's and d'Alembert's *Encyclopédie* (1751–1772), which is accompanied by the following warning: "One must take special care to avoid

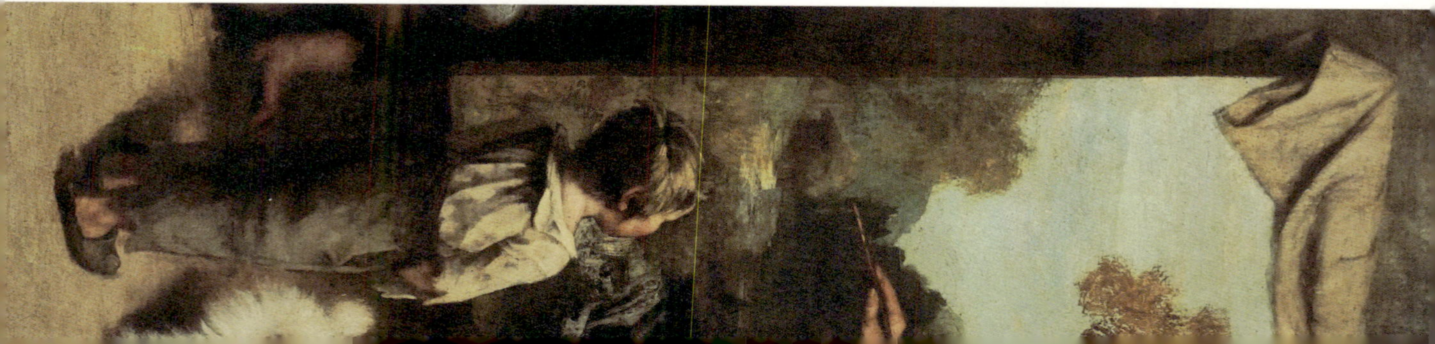

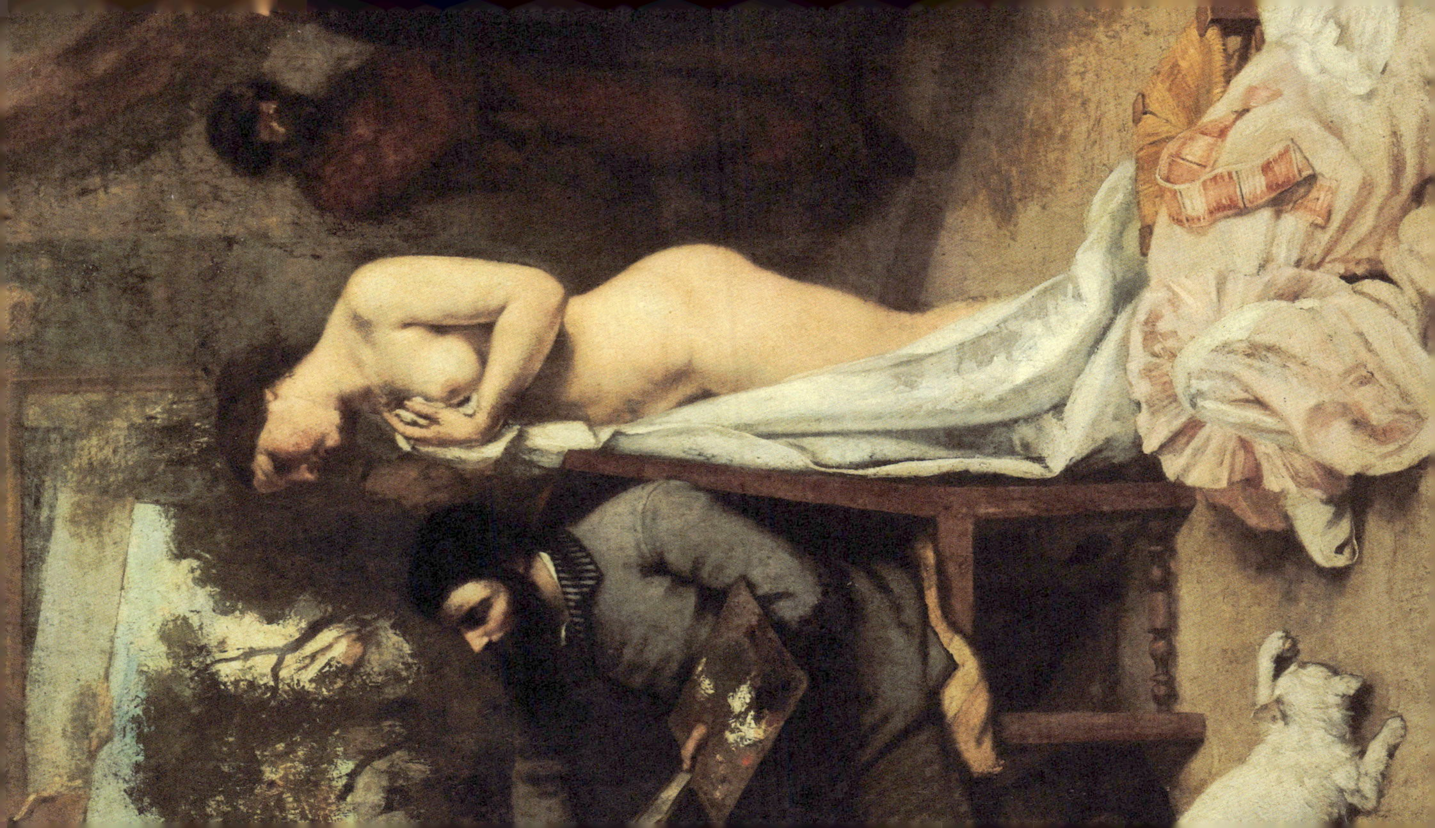

ambiguity when talking to children, who should be raised with an unequivocal and clear language." Did Delacroix use the word "amphibologie" in this sense? Perhaps he is referring to the boy in *The Artist's Studio,* who watches the painter at work and recalls the inquisitive boy from *The Wheat Sifters,* whom we discussed in the previous chapter (ill. p. 44/45). The child's observation of the artwork should not, Delacroix seems to argue, be misled by the charade of a "real sky." For Delacroix, ambiguity in art was to be avoided. For Courbet, by contrast, ambiguity was programmatic: the boy's spontaneous, uncorrupted glance inaugurates a completely new way of accessing art; new, logically inexplicable pictorial levels open up.

Courbet has illustrated a modernist myth here: the dispassionate, unadulterated viewing of art, unspoiled by the constraints of tradition. The other figures from the central group in the *Studio* can also be interpreted in this regard. At first there is the painter himself, who, as he wrote to Champfleury, depicted himself with his "Assyrian profile." This refers to the shape of his beard, which resembles the stylized facial hair familiar from Assyrian art. Courbet, who was very vain, was particularly proud of his supposedly Assyrian appearance. "Assyrian"—for Courbet, this also meant an archaic art form that was not oriented toward the idealized body of classical antiquity and the Renaissance. Courbet has depicted himself in the moment of creation: with his brush in his right hand, he paints a landscape whose sky Delacroix deemed so lifelike that he felt compelled to criticize it in the manner described above. The elementary means assisting him in the creative act are the painter's instruments he holds in his hands as well as the pure material, the paint on his palette, which he ennobles by turning it into art.

The cat playing in the foreground surely represents an animalism far removed from the civilized world, but it can also be understood as an allusion to unbridled sexuality. In French, the female form of the word cat, "la chatte," is a colloquial term for vulva. And what about the woman Delacroix believed to have been painted so extraordinarily well by Courbet? She stands behind the painter and looks—quite clearly—less at the painting itself than at the hand that paints it, and consequently at the process of the genesis of art. She is depicted as a real woman who uncloaks her real body to reveal her natural beauty. Can she be associated with "Nuda veritas," the naked truth? If so, she would have no need to hold a sheet before her body. Does the painting suggest that both the act of artistic creation and human procreation always require the erotic game of veiling and unveiling?

All considerations ultimately return to the insight that everything is painting: the woman's painted sheet and clothing that flow from the painted landscape like a painted waterfall;[52] the landscape painted by the artist, who simultaneously paints his self-portrait and the very colors he used to paint this picture. *The Artist's Studio* contains yet another level: there is another artist who is also at work here. A boy visible to the right of the central group lies on the floor and draws (ill. p. 65). We cannot see what he is drawing, but here again we witness a child's insouciant access to art: Was Courbet using this figure to call into question the academic ideal of illusionistic perfection, the lack of which Delacroix criticized in *A Burial?*

When contemplating *The Artist's Studio,* one should always keep in mind the manifesto of artistic intentions with which Courbet prefaced the catalogue of his 1855 exhibition:[53] "J'ai voulu tout simplement puiser dans l'entière connaissance de la tradition le sentiment raisonné et indépendant de ma propre individualité" ["I have simply wanted to draw from a thorough knowledge of tradition the reasoned and free sense of my own individuality"].

Rarely has the individuality of the artist—grounded in tradition but fundamentally independent—been emphasized to the extent that Courbet does here. He does not regard himself as an aloof artist-genius in the traditional sense, defined by academic standards and guided by "higher powers." He knows all about tradition but is obliged solely to himself in all his doings. This artist's self-portrait remains decisive today. Was Courbet, the individualist and avant-gardist who depicted the confusingly multifaceted, irrational possibilities of a painting, the first or at least one of the first modern artists?

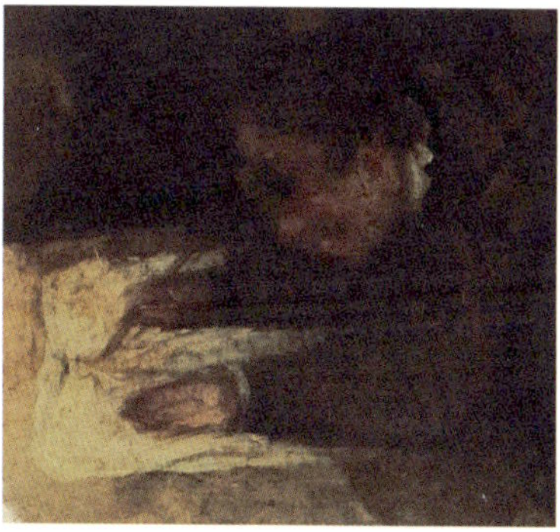

Courbet produced almost all of his self-portraits between 1840 and 1855. They played a crucial role at a time when Courbet was establishing himself in Paris as the leading painter of Realism and the artist who was always good for a scandal: Courbet developed the expressive possibilities of his paintings in dialogue with his own physical appearance.[54] The various poses and roles he assumed in them should be seen as self-imposed tasks, and one can understand why he kept many of these pictures for himself, holding on to them for the rest of his life as documents of his artistic journey. His remark in a letter to Alfred Bruyas, that he had written an autobiography in self-portraits, should be understood in this particular light.[55] Aside from the technical challenges posed by his self-portraits—he never had any regular academic training—they can also be regarded figuratively as stages on the path to artistic individuality, and as he announced in the programmatic text to his 1855 exhibition, discussed in the previous chapter, it was to this individuality alone that Courbet felt himself obliged.

Facing up to his individuality as an artist, fully aware of tradition but nevertheless relying solely on himself: this was risky business. I believe that Courbet made it the subject of one of his self-portraits, known since the 1882 sales exhibition of works from his studio as *Le fou de peur* (*The Man Mad with Fear*, ca. 1848, ill. p. 69).[56] He apparently showed the picture in 1855 under the title *Le suicide, paysage de 1848* in his "Pavilion of Realism" adjacent to the Exposition Universelle in Paris. There was no indication that it was an oil sketch or other unfinished work.[57] Hence, there is much to be said for the assumption that Courbet regarded this painting as a fully valid, completed work.

The picture shows an artist in a sunny landscape. He is wearing a striped jacket with a cape affixed to his left shoulder. He seems to want to stand up; he reaches out with his right hand into the foreground and places his left hand flat on his head. The artist's face indicates great desperation, as if he were having a horrific vision. Some commentators have even wanted to see an abyss below him—one into which he will plummet at any moment.

Courbet frequently overpainted or reworked his paintings. Thanks to X-ray technology, it has become possible to reconstruct the artist's "lost" oeuvre, as it were.[58] Under the surface of his 1853 painting *Baigneuses* (*Bathers*, Musée Fabre, Montpellier), for example, traces of two other pictures are discernible: *L'homme délivré de l'amour par la mort (Man Delivered from Love by Death)*, an allegorical painting from the mid-eighteen-forties, and *La nuit classique de Walpurgis (Classical Walpurgis Night)* from 1848, which references a scene from Johann Wolfgang von Goethe's *Faust Part Two*.[59] The respective upper sections of these super-

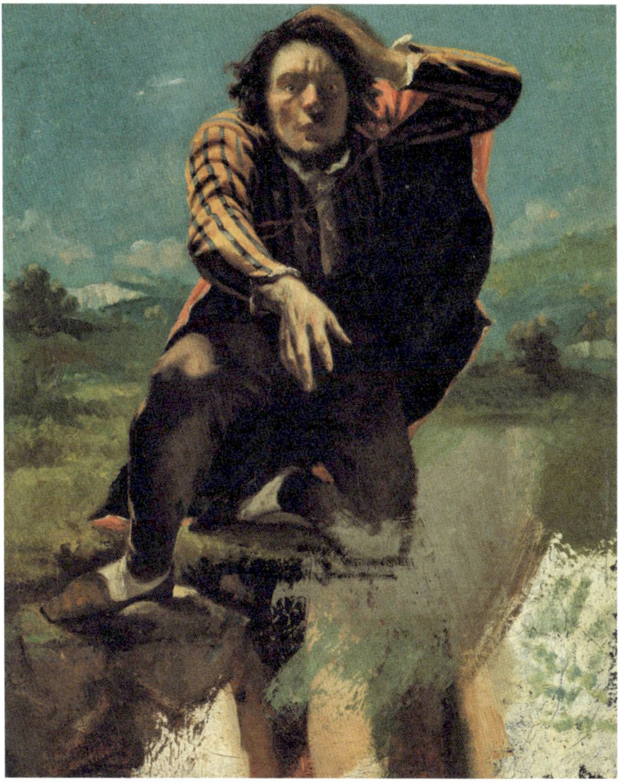

Gustave Courbet, *Portrait de l'artiste*, known as *Le fou de peur (Portrait of the Artist*, known as *The Man Mad with Fear)*, ca. 1848, oil on paper on canvas, 60.5 × 50.5 cm, The National Museum of Art, Architecture, and Design, Oslo imposed pictorial ideas are dominated by a figure resembling the man made mad by fear, which was evidently a preparatory study for it. The overpainted pictures located under the surface of *Baigneuses* seem to depict someone pursuing a woman—for example, Faust in search of Helena in the second part of Goethe's tragedy. Courbet was apparently convinced that he could exhibit the motif on its own, without any obvious connections to literary content.

Whether the artist meant to depict someone who has been made mad with fear, a would-be suicide, or someone trailing behind a chimera is not entirely clear. What is decisive about this picture is that Courbet has depicted himself as someone plunging into an abyss constituted by free painting. In the lower, uncompleted passage of picture, as it were, Courbet seems to be completely alone as a painter. One sees the artist's hand in the truest sense of the word here: on the white fleck at the lower right one can almost see the outline of a hand with splayed fingers—probably meant to represent a *painted* handprint.[60]

I interpret this picture programmatically: Courbet depicts himself as someone plunging into something entirely new. Is it death? Or is it a new sort of painting into which Courbet, detached as he is from the academic tradition, casts himself? This can be very frightening; it is almost like a suicide—particularly when things go wrong; the brutal criticism reaped by works exhibited by Courbet shortly thereafter might have driven an artist with less self-confidence to put an end to his life.

In *The Artist's Studio* (ill. p. 54/55), Courbet portrayed himself as the painter of a landscape. Does this mean that he intended to concentrate more on landscape painting after working on the large programmatic pictures of Realism? This assumption is confirmed by consulting the catalogue raisonné of his works. Most of the pictures produced by Courbet after 1855 are landscapes; by then he had already painted his realistic masterpieces. Landscapes in particular offered him the possibility of demonstrating his artistic individuality. They also sold well—Courbet's style became a brand for which there was a demand.[61]

Courbet's individuality is strongly expressed in his technique: one must keep in mind that nineteenth-century audiences paid much more attention to *how* a painting was made than does today's public. In the early nineteenth century, a "completed" painting had to represent an idea, not call attention to the artist's hand and by extension to the artist himself. It was acceptable to the public, for example, if an artist exhibited a picture and declared it to be a sketch that showed a personal brushwork style. But what was not accepted was when such sketch-like paintings were officially presented as fully valid, completed works of art.[62] Courbet was one of the painters who broke these rules. But it would be increasingly tolerated—particularly in the area of landscape painting.

Courbet used paint as a material in a manner that was completely unconventional for his day.[63] The aforementioned Alexandre Schanne (see p. 36/37) recalls Courbet's exceptional technique, which he probably saw during the eighteen-forties in the studio of "Père Lapin," where one could work after a nude model for six francs a month:

> He [Courbet] painted on thick gray paper primed with oil that was stretched on a framework three times larger in size than normal canvases. . . . The box he made use of had an unusual size, containing enormous containers full of the most conventional colors that one could buy by the kilo; white, yellow ochre, vermillion, black. . . . He mixed his colors after thoroughly observing the model: he prepared three basic tones, one for light, one for highlighting and one for shadow. He then distributed the fresh paint in a fan-like manner on his palette. After he did that, he painted with brushes, with palette knives, with rags and even with his thumbs; everything suited him. But he occupied himself more with the harmony of the colors than with their richness, a characteristic that he incidentally retained until the end of his career. Nobody ever saw him execute a whole figure in Father Lapin's studio; he only studied a section.[64]

But it was Courbet's intense use of the palette knife in particular that was spectacular. A palette knife is like a small trowel with which the artist smoothes the paint on his picture, giving the impression that is was not so much painted as constructed in overlapping layers of color.[65] This technique as employed by Courbet is still admired by painters today—for example, Peter

Doig (born 1959), who once stated that Courbet molded more than painted.[66] And Paul Cézanne (1839–1906) described admiringly how Courbet "slapped paint on the way a plasterer slaps on stucco . . . He built like a Roman mason."[67] When Adolph Menzel (1815–1905), another contemporary, met Courbet in Paris in 1867 (and acquired a painting from him for his own collection[68]), he is supposed to have said that one should take away all of Courbet's brushes because he is "excellent" so long as he paints with a palette knife.[69] And Gerhard Richter (born 1932), who rubbed and scraped layers of paint over the surface of his abstract pictures with a squeegee, owes much to Courbet's palette knife technique. Following the precedent of his nineteenth-century role model, Richter even named two abstract pictures "A B, Courbet" in 1986.[70] Courbet is by all means an artist's artist: Pablo Picasso (1881–1973) at any rate owned one of his works, and Henri Matisse (1869–1954) owned at least four. Perhaps the true significance of Courbet's legacy rests more in his liberated handling of paint than in his monumental realist canvases; their impressiveness cannot be denied, but their original social explosiveness is difficult to comprehend today.

Courbet's use of everyday prefabricated paint recalls the way Jackson Pollock (1912–1956) painted with automotive lacquer, and Courbet did not tinker about with paint like Paul Klee did. He seems not to have attached any importance to the quality of the paint he worked with; speed is what mattered to him, and paint had to be available in large quantities so he could

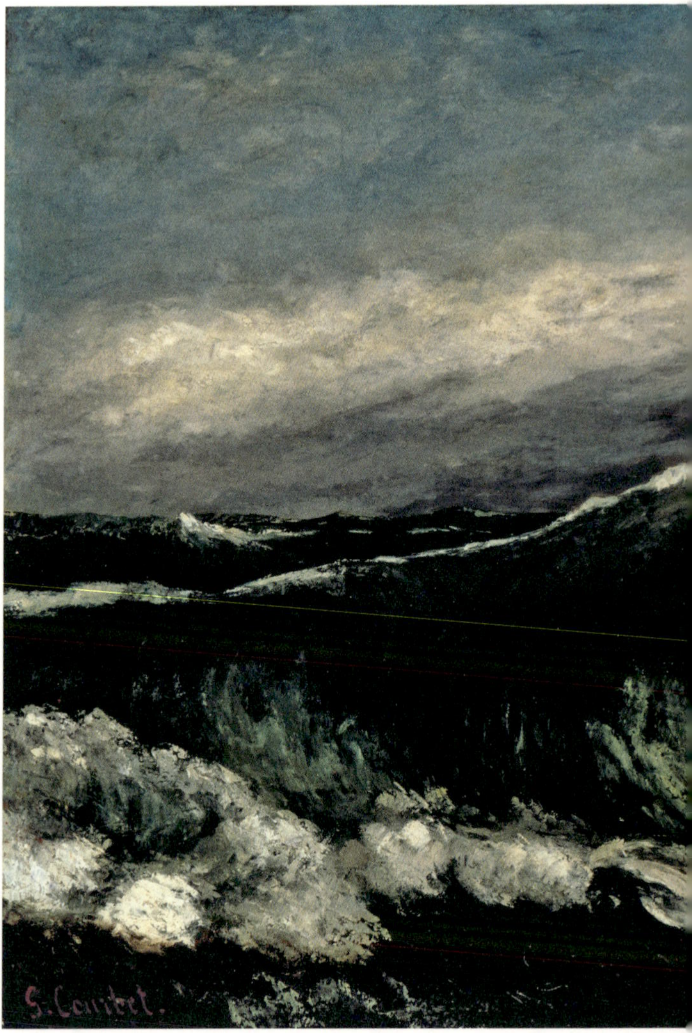

Gustave Courbet, *La vague (The Wave)*, ca. 1869, oil on canvas, 65.4 × 88.7 cm, Brooklyn Museum, New York, Gift of Mrs. Horace Havemeyer

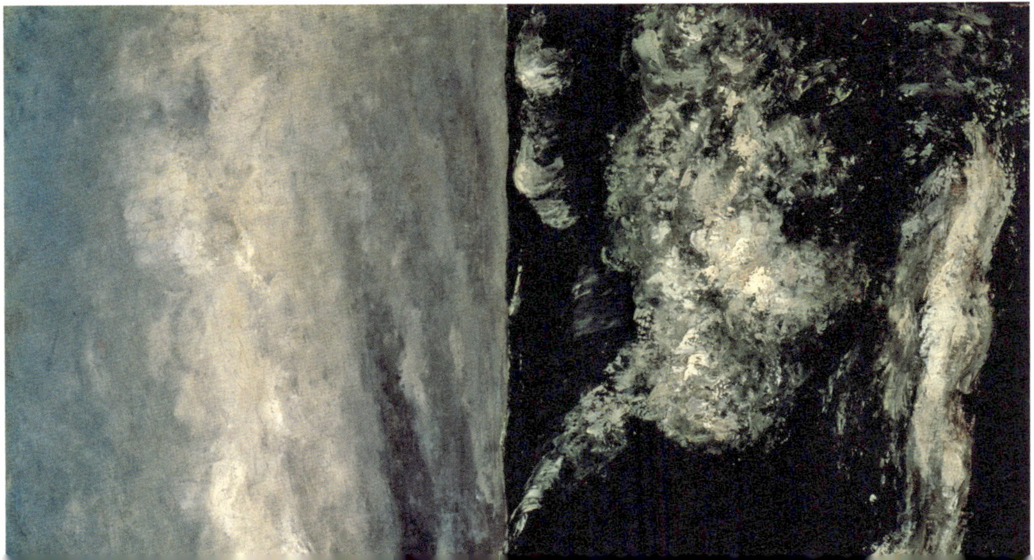

apply it in thick layers. This made it possible for him to work fast, something that was particularly useful in the case of his famed depictions of waves (ill. p. 74/75), because he wanted to capture the exact moment when the wave crashed onto the shore. The writer Guy de Maupassant once described how he observed Courbet painting waves at Étretat on the Atlantic coast in 1869. Courbet was living in a house in the immediate vicinity of the water's edge and his window opened onto the storm-tossed sea nearby. The painter frequently looked out of the window, returning to his canvas a moment later in order to smear thick globs of paint onto the canvas with a kitchen knife.[71] Maupassant was not one of Courbet's biggest fans, having elsewhere described the artist as unkempt and loud. And it is questionable whether Courbet really used a kitchen knife. In any case, the caricaturist Amédée de Noé (1819–1879), known as Cham, published a drawing of a wave by Courbet in 1870: it shows a hand holding a large knife on which there is a breaking wave.[72] A close look at the actual pictures reveals—as one might expect—that Courbet sometimes had to wait until a layer of paint was dry in order to add the foam to a painted wave, for example, because the colors would otherwise have blended together.[73] Similarly, the diverse hues of green, gray, and blue from which the waves are constructed cannot have been smeared onto a canvas in a matter of seconds with a kitchen knife.

Courbet himself contributed to his mythical status as a "fast painter." It is reported that he boasted to Adolph Menzel—whom, as mentioned above, he encountered in 1867—about how

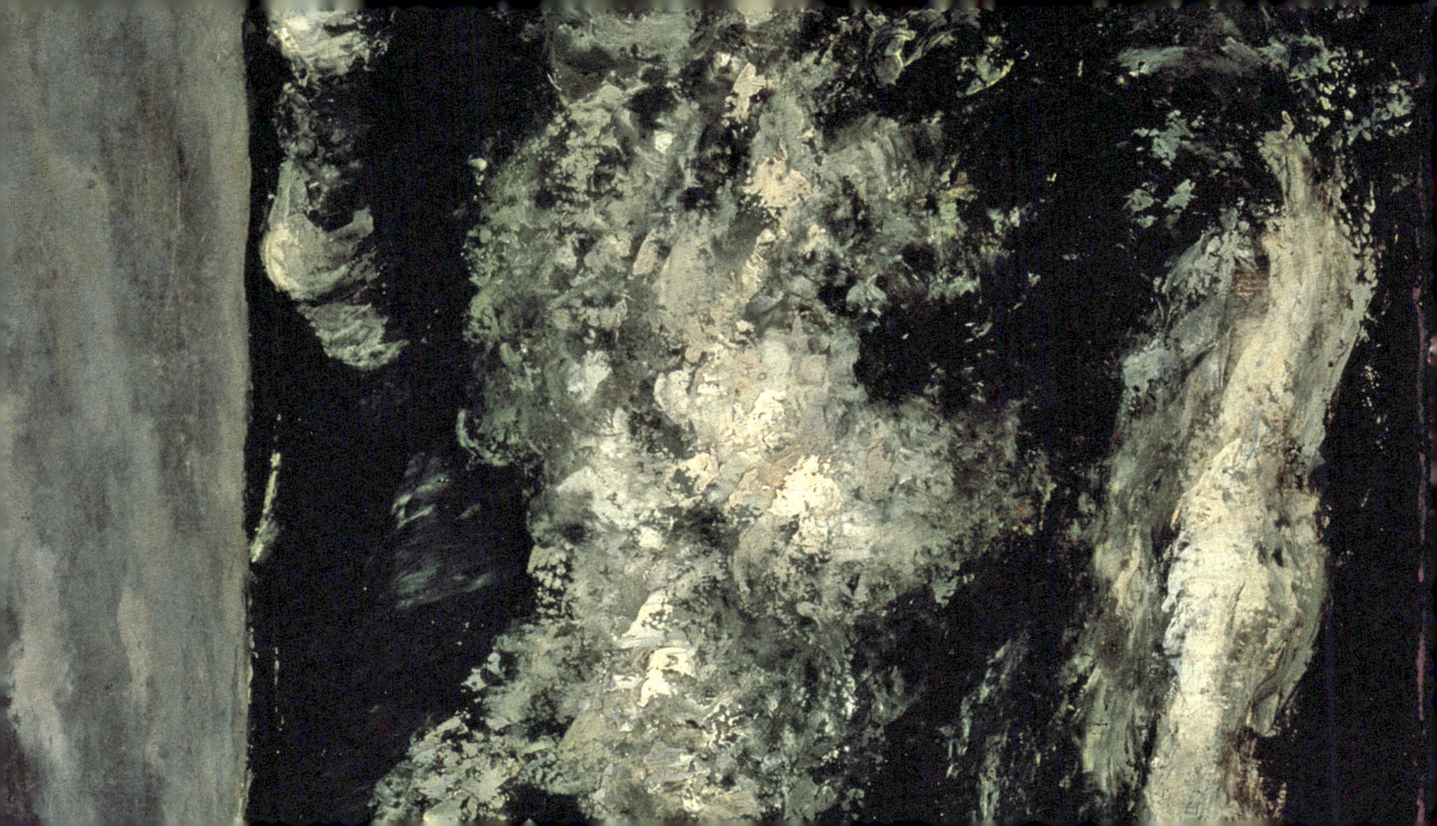

fast he could paint his seascapes, alluding to his paintings with views in the distance of a peaceful body of water, a cloudless sky, or an approaching storm. This account was provided by the now largely forgotten genre painter Paul Friedrich Meyerheim (1842–1915), who accompanied Menzel:

> He [Courbet] related that he once painted three or four maritime picture in one day. He mixes a large heap of paint as the tone for the air and then spreads it with his palette knife all the way across the painting. He then does the same with the tone for water and, if necessary, the sand at the front. He drastically demonstrates the spreading motion for us, gesticulating with his thumbs in the air. He then places the sails, the seagulls, the edges of the waves, the ships etc. with the paintbrush. The truth of the tones in these maritime pictures, however, has something remarkable and fresh about it.[74]

Three tones in combination with the gesture of painting result in pictures that today count among Courbet's most beautiful and atmospheric works. It is interesting to note that Meyerheim first talks about tones and then mentions that sand is applied in front if necessary. He meant the color used for sand; naturally Courbet did not paint with actual sand. But this touches on an important point: as paradoxical as it sounds, color is equivalent to the depicted material in Courbet's paintings and vice versa. This is particularly true in the pictures of waves, where the apparent transformation of color into form results in such direct and outwardly three-dimensional results that it occasioned Paul Cézanne to declare: "It hits you right in the stomach. You have to step back. The entire room feels the spray."[75] As regards the wave preserved at the Musée d'Orsay, Joan Miró (1893–1983) similarly remarked, "Even if this painting had been behind our backs, we would have felt it."[76]

One final example: a large proportion of Courbet's landscapes are dedicated to the depiction of his native region. Anyone who has ever visited this area—with its plateaus transversed by deeply carved valleys, its spectacular rock formations, its dark and secretive watercourses, and its enormous grottos from whence water dashes forth from the sources of the rivers—will understand how well qualified Courbet was to portray the landscape's geological structures, because he seems to have shaped them in paint.[77] In Courbet's 1864 painting of a grotto and the source of a river, probably the Lison, the spatial impact of the overlapping layers of sedimentation is nothing less than amazing (ill. p. 80). The closer the viewer comes to the painting, the more everything dissolves into clearly distinguishable brushstrokes: as if geology and painting were congruent.

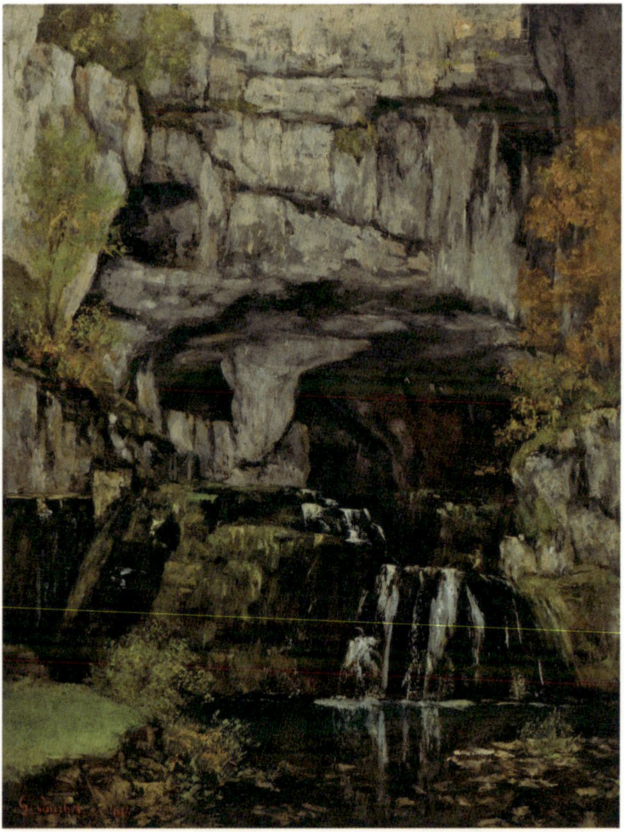

Gustave Courbet, *Source du Lison (Source of the Lison)*, 1864, oil on canvas, 91 × 73 cm, private collection

Origine du monde – Origine de la peinture

In 1855, the year Courbet exhibited his *Painter's Studio* (showing him at work on a landscape) in a separate pavilion adjacent to the Parisian Exposition Universelle, he was also represented in the art section of the official show with eleven paintings that had been accepted by the jury. They included a relatively large-format work entitled *Le ruisseau du Puits-Noir, vallée de la Loue* (*Stream of the Puits-Noir, Loue Valley*, ill. p. 82/83), which is unusual in many respects: we see an uninhabited forest landscape with the rocky walls of a gorge and a stream; a small section of blue sky is visible above. The eye, however, is not directed towards a middle point, as is the case in traditional landscapes. The viewer slowly discerns the course taken by the stream as it disappears into the background. The painting makes a very dark impression, one that is more than just a consequence of the aging process: anyone who has ever wandered here himself is aware of how dark, how utterly uncanny these quiet valleys in the vicinity of Ornans are. Dark flecks in the painting, baffling light-absorbing zones in the water, are quite conspicuous. It just so happens that the depicted site is called "Puits-Noir," i.e. "Black Well," a name deriving from special characteristics of the Jura's limestone landscape. Water seeps into the countless

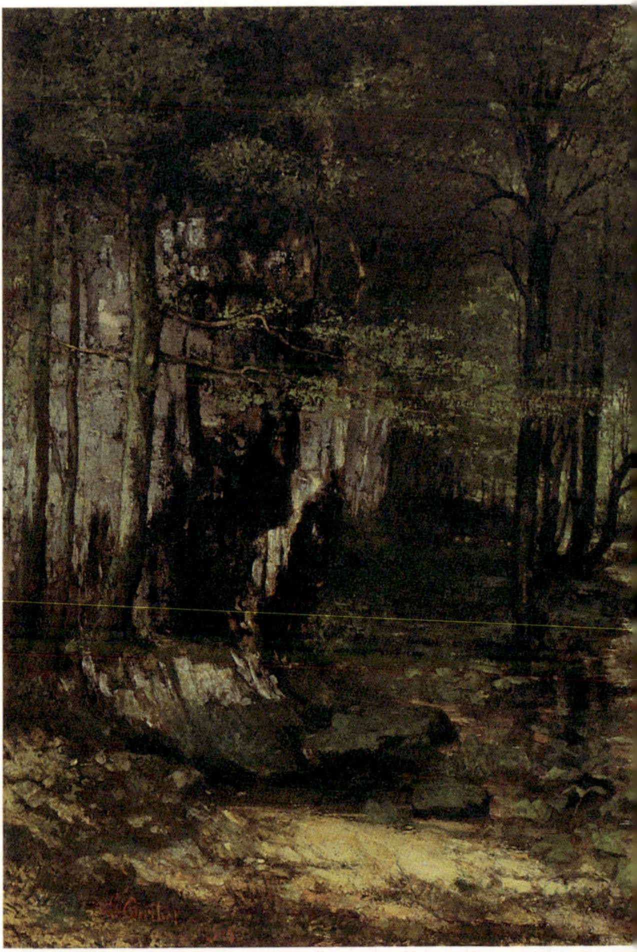

Gustave Courbet, *Le ruisseau du Puits-Noir, vallée de la Loue (The Stream of the Puits-Noir, Loue Valley)*, 1855, oil on canvas, 104 × 137 cm, National Gallery of Art, Washington DC, Gift of Mr. and Mrs. P.H.B. Freylinghuysen in memory of her father and mother, Mr. and Mrs. H.O. Havemeyer

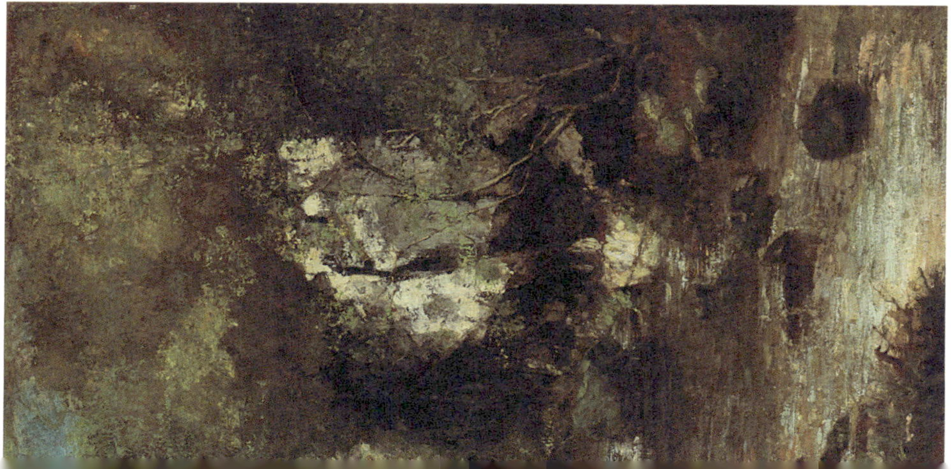

subterranean caves and emerges again from seemingly unfathomable depths. In this painting Courbet has erected a kind of monument to the special physiographic features of his native region.

There are also dark zones in Courbet's paintings of grottos and sources, most of which were made in 1864. Flowing from impenetrable depths, water issues from these caves in the center of the pictures. If we interpret the grotto paintings as an attempt to achieve something like congruence between geological formations and painting, then the omission of the center emphasizes the immense spatial depths of the hollows. Visitors to the sources of the Loue and Lison rivers or the Grotto of Sarrazine are amazed by the domes of rock that tower above if one assumes positions corresponding to those taken by Courbet when he painted these pictures. The dark zones in the middle of Courbet's cave paintings seem to draw the viewer's gaze into the interior of the rock openings. The grottos make an archaic impression.

The black flecks, the obscure centers in Courbet's pictures, are very closely associated with the artist's concept of painting, which is surely shaped by the notion that black is the starting point of art. Courbet almost always painted on darkly primed canvases; in this sense he adopted an approach entirely in keeping with the old masters. There is an account stating that he believed nature to be black and obscure without sunlight. As a painter he acts as light does: he illuminates what protrudes from on high and the painting is finished.[78] In this sense all of his grotto scenes are manifestos of painting; the dark centers show unlit nature, the point from which Courbet developed his paintings.

Black, absolute darkness, and white, absolute brightness, represent the two extremes of the color scale. While it is true that Courbet made opaque darkness the subject of many of his paintings, he was also an eminent painter of white, and in fact it would be correct to say that white takes on a very special, nearly three-dimensional quality in his winter pictures. Here too the materiality of the color seems to correspond to the materiality of snow. One example is *Braconniers dans la neige* (*Poachers in the Snow*, ill. p. 86/87). It is one of the most important hunting scenes ever painted by Courbet, who was a passionate hunter himself. The painting, which dates from 1867, shows a blinding white snowfield across which two hunters walk with their dogs. One of the men threatens his dog with a stick, probably by way of forcing the animal to take up the trail of the game whose tracks are visible in the snow. There is also snow on the boots of the poachers: white paint, thickly applied, assumes the characteristics of snow. A true-to-life depiction of snow-covered boots would arrive at a different result, but surely one that is not as convincing. The paint, the snow, covers all traces; the manner in which it outshines everything makes it just as impenetrable as its opposite on the other end of the color scale. Its brilliant brightness causes the men—dark figures in every sense of the word—to appear particularly obscure, endowing the scene as a whole with something archaic, something

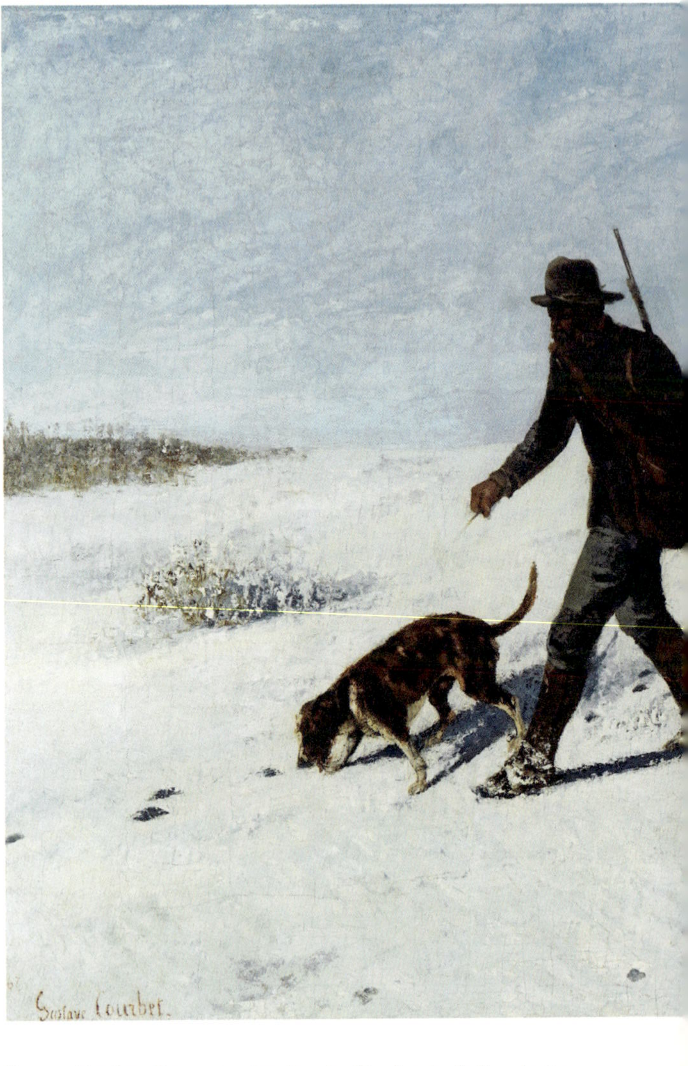

Gustave Courbet, ***Braconniers dans la neige (Poachers in the Snow)***, 1867, oil on canvas, 102 × 122 cm, Galleria Nazionale d'Arte Moderna, Rome

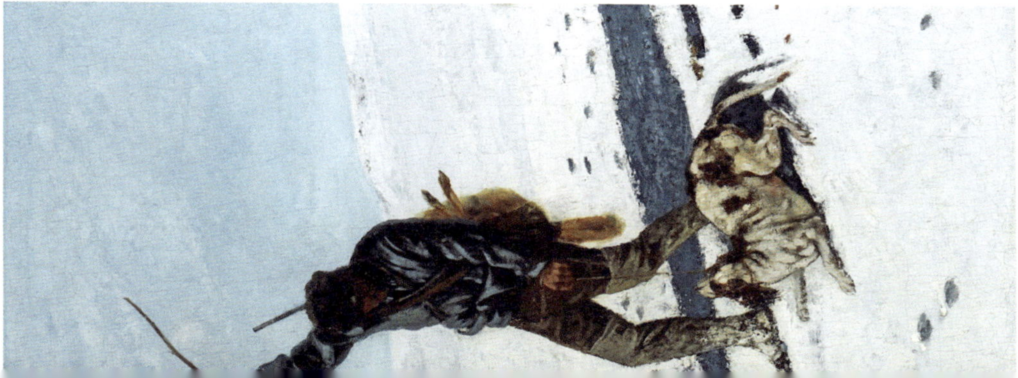

frightening. It is wonderful to observe how Courbet depicts the fabric of the jacket worn by the poacher on the right, which shimmers in the light between shadow and blue, with only a few blue brushstrokes. It is not surprising that the circle of young painters around Claude Monet (1840–1926), who were later designated Impressionists, were particularly impressed by the radiant white in these pictures.[79]

Let us return to the dark, light-absorbing zones: areas of black resembling black springs can also be seen in Courbet's famous paintings of nude women at ponds and streams. *La jeune baigneuse* (*The Bather*, ill. p. 90) from 1866 is one example: the water into which she cautiously steps is abysmally dark. What is this woman, who is holding onto a branch that is much too thin, doing at the waterside? Is she washing her feet while completely undressed? And what about the woman with black hair in the painting *Trois baigneuses* (*Three Bathers*, ill. p. 15), who is being helped into the water—inky black, of course—where a redheaded beauty awaits her. What is the point of all that? And why do Courbet's paintings feature so many undressed women sleeping near shady forest springs or letting water run over their arms?

Grottos and springs also have a symbolic meaning in Courbet's work, particularly in conjunction with the depiction of nude women. Many grottos in his native region were called "Dames"—ladies.[80] Has the painter been influenced by the folklore of the Franche-Comté? The omnipresence of water, the mysteriousness of the springs and waterfalls, are also reflected in local legends. The mythological world of Franche-Comté is peopled by witches, by "green" and "white ladies"—usually breathtakingly beautiful but dangerous fairies and nymphs that live in or near grottos and springs and terrorize lonely travelers.[81] Should Courbet's paintings depicting nude women near forest springs be viewed against this backdrop? The 1868 painting *La source* (*The Source*, ill. p. 91), one of Courbet's last female nudes, can be interpreted as follows: the woman who turns her back to the viewer and lets water run over her left hand is in truth a seductive water nymph whose actual countenance will frighten the viewer when she turns around to faces him. It is particularly worthy of note in this work that the bather's face—or at least that part of it which we should be able to see because she has turned her head somewhat to the left—has been left undefined, as if the painting were in fact unfinished.

There is a long art-historical tradition of representing water nymphs and women near water. One only has to think of Jean-Auguste-Dominique Ingres's *La source* from 1856, a picture of an ethereal young woman without pubic hair who carries on her left shoulder an amphora from which she pours water into a pond that is as smooth as a mirror. In 1866 a successful ballet by Ludwig Minkus and Léo Delibes called *La source* premiered in Paris; it would become the subject of an 1868 painting by Edgar Degas (1834–1917). With the exception of the *Bathers* from 1853, Courbet's pictures of women near water were painted around the same time; the extent to which there might be a connection to Ingres's famous painting is uncertain. In any case,

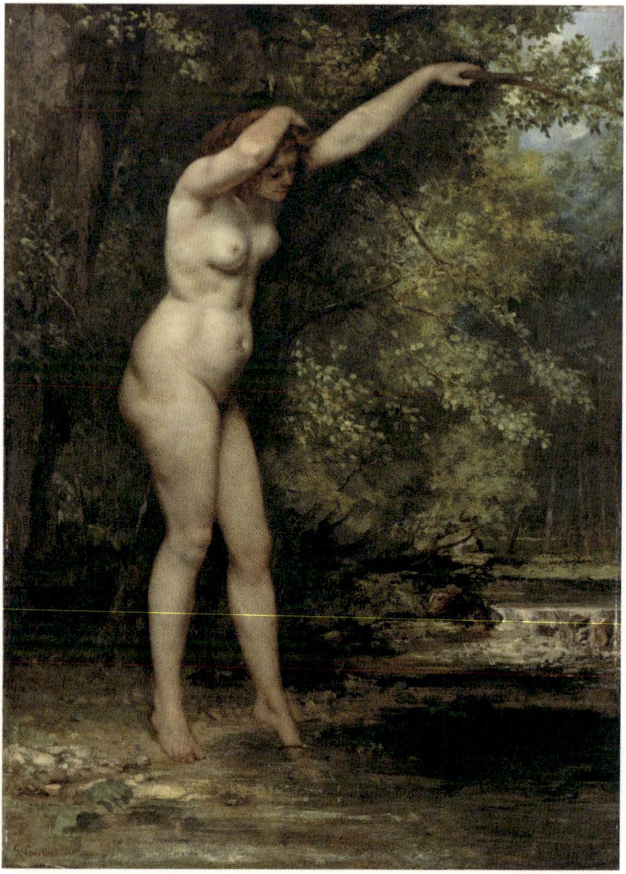

Gustave Courbet, ***La jeune baigneuse (The Bather)***, 1866,
oil on canvas, 130.2 × 97.2 cm, The Metropolitan Museum of Art, New York,
The Havemeyer Collection, Bequest of Mrs. H.O. Havemeyer

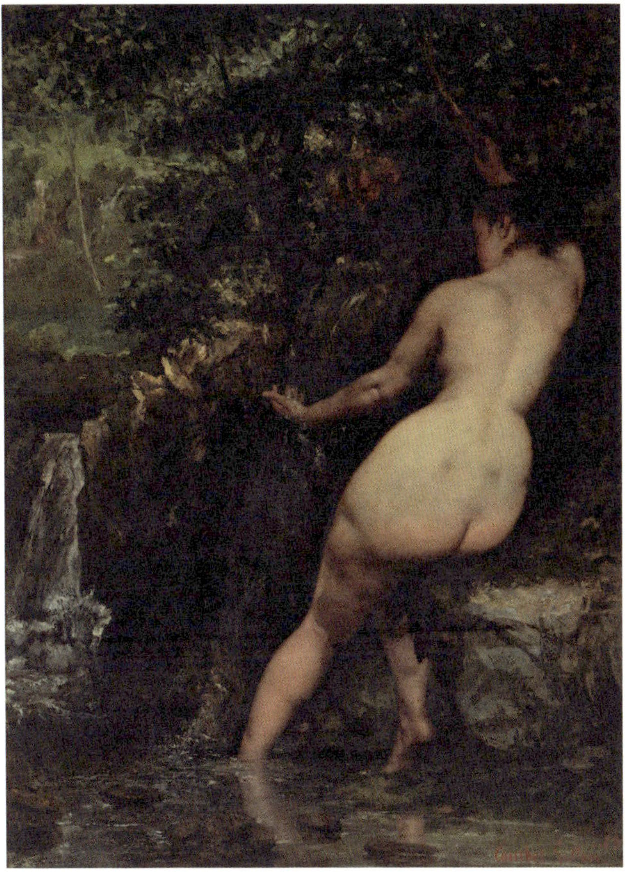

Gustave Courbet, *La source (The Source)*, 1868, oil on canvas, 128 × 97.5 cm, Musée d'Orsay, Paris they seem to emphasize the erotic component inherent in the combination of spring and woman: Are these paintings of women entering deep, unfathomable bodies of water more or less overt depictions of sexual initiation? Can we consider them allegories of sexuality?

The nineteenth century, which was virtually obsessed by (mostly) male sexual fantasies, developed an extensive apparatus for depicting them more or less openly. Courbet was a great master of erotic allusion, and naturally this also encompasses the fact that his grotto paintings can be interpreted as anthropomorphic landscapes—even without the depiction of women. Do the grottos allude to female genitals?[82]

One painting in particular gives rise to these ideas: Courbet's *L'origine du monde* (*The Origin of the World,* 1866, ill. p. 94/95)—famous and scandalous in equal measure—which quite graphically represents a woman's genitals, parts of her thighs, and a breast.[83] Courbet painted the picture for the Egyptian diplomat Khalil Bey. As a part of his notorious collection of erotic art, the painting was concealed behind a green curtain, which he drew back only for the delectation of selected guests—for example, after dinner, when the host retired with his visitors for the more informal part of the evening. This, in any case, is how the situation was described by the author and librettist Ludovic Halévy. The politician Léon Gambetta, a friend of Courbet's, told Halévy about a stag party at Khalil Bey's home, which the painter also attended. The company viewed Courbet's masterpiece after dinner, with each guest outdoing the other in their praise and admiration for the painting and—we can assume—for its subject matter as well. Only the painter remained silent for a long time, until he finally remarked: "You think this beautiful . . . and you are right. . . . Yes, it is very beautiful, and listen, Titian, Veronese, their Raphael, I myself, none of us have ever done anything more beautiful. . . ."[84]

It is an impressive example of Courbet's outspoken self-confidence: he was well aware that he had not only broken a taboo with this painting, but also put an end to centuries of suggestive sexual allusions—as if the picture were a painted: "Well, so what?" In this sense the work likewise alludes to the scandalous *Olympia*, painted by Courbet's rival Edouard Manet (1832–1883) in 1863 and exhibited in 1865, which shows a reclining nude prostitute who, like Titian's *Venus of Urbino*, covers her genitals with one of her hands.

But let us return to Khalil Bey's stag party: after dinner the host unveiled the painting, surely with a flair for the dramatic, that in turn depicts someone who is herself partially veiled or unveiled, depending on how one looks at it. The energetically painted white garment appears to have ridden up her body or been turned back. The model's genitals are unveiled by the painter; her personality, however, remains obscure. As was already the case in *The Painter's Studio* (ill. p. 54/55), Courbet seems to be playing once again with the motif of dressing and undressing.

There is a prior art-historical precedent for a work that, like this picture, depicts a woman whose genitals are uncovered but

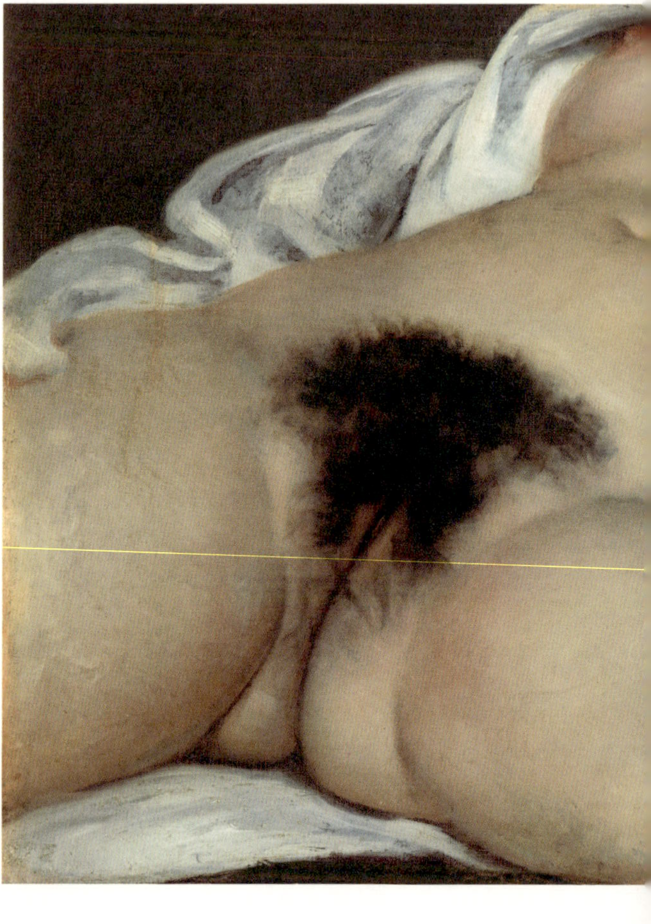

Gustave Courbet, *L'origine du monde (The Origin of the World)*, 1866, oil on canvas, 46 × 55 cm, Musée d'Orsay, Paris

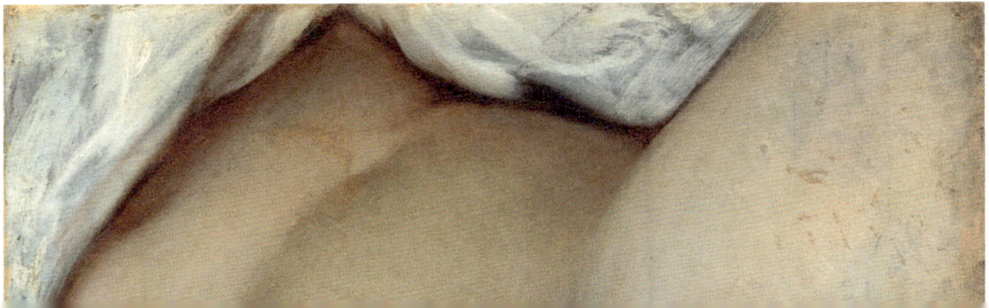

whose identity remains concealed. In Eugène Delacroix' sophisticated small-format painting *The Duke of Orléans Showing His Lover to the Duke of Burgundy* (ill. p. 97), a man disrobes the lower section of a woman's body in front of another man, who, in the context of the picture, cannot see her face, although it is quite visible for us as viewers of the entire work. Similarly, the viewer within the picture can see her genitals while we, viewers of the painting, cannot. The risqué part of this scene, which is probably based on a story from *Les Vies des dames galantes* by Pierre de Bourdeille, Seigneur de Brantôme (ca. 1540–1614), is that the viewer in the painting is the husband of the partially disrobed woman, whom—in his enthusiasm for her private parts—he does not recognize. Courbet can conceivably have seen this painting in 1864, when it was probably sold at a Parisian auction.[85]

It is important to note that Courbet's painting depicts—one might also say unveils—the female genitals as such. However, it is not correct to speak of the "de-individualization" of the woman in this connection. Courbet seems to be more concerned with an overriding principle—namely, the origin of the world, which from his perspective is female. The painting was already titled *L'origine du monde* when Léon Gambetta viewed it together with Courbet; the name seems to have come from the artist himself. It is probably the title in particular that also establishes a link to the paintings of the grottos in Courbet's native region, to the extent that the viewer is even overcome by the feeling of being at places where world has given birth to itself.

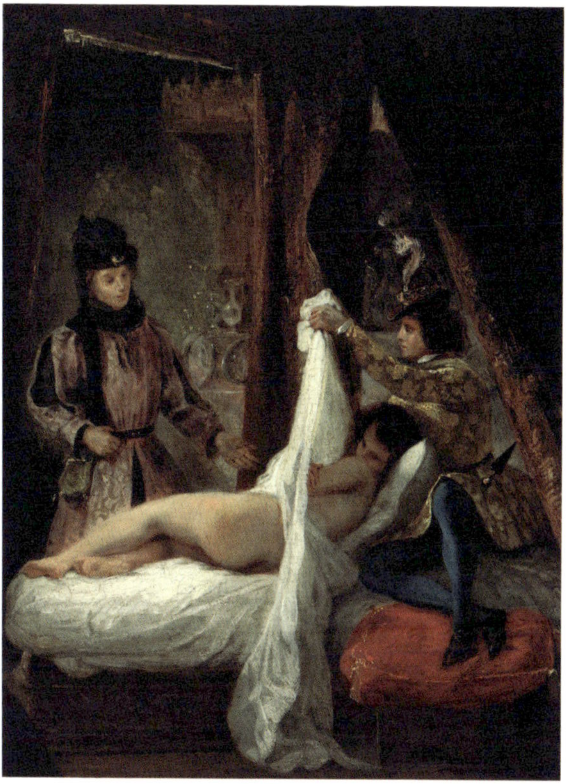

Eugène Delacroix, *Le Duc d'Orléans montrant sa maitresse au Duc de Bourgogne (The Duke of Orléans Showing His Lover to the Duke of Burgundy)*, ca. 1825/26, oil on canvas, 35 × 25.5 cm, Museo Thyssen-Bornemisza, Madrid

L'origine du monde had the honor of being the most famous unseen painting of the nineteenth century, a veritable "chef d'œuvre inconnu" and source of inspiration for artists up to the present day.[86] One knew of the painting and spoke about it without ever having seen it. A caricature was even published in 1867 that showed Courbet standing before a painting on which only a fig leaf is visible—a definite allusion to a painting that is by no means an allusion itself.

Yet surely the painting is an allusion to the extent that it depicts the female genitals but does not represent sexuality. It does not show what—possibly—plays out in the mind of the viewer: the glance is drawn into the darkness of the pubic hair and beyond the labia, into the unfathomable darkness of painting. This brings us back to the grottos, which are perhaps not so much metaphors for the vulva as for the abysses of sexuality, which cannot be illustrated. Like the grotto paintings, *L'origine du monde* may also be a manifesto of art and its manifold possibilities. In this sense, the origin of the world is also the origin of art.

Epilogue

Gustave Courbet was a broken man when he died at the age of fifty-eight in the company of his aged father on December 31, 1877, at La Tour-de-Peilz on Lake Geneva. Old before his time, he had grown heavy, was addicted to the bottle, and moreover suffered from homesickness. He went into exile in Switzerland in July 1873 to avoid prosecution by the French criminal authorities. Courbet had participated actively in politics after the collapse of the Second Empire in 1870 and during the 1871 Paris Commune; among other things, he had been elected president of the commission tasked with protecting the public art collections. After the bloody suppression of the Commune, reactionary forces within France's bourgeoisie seem finally to have found a cause with which they could avenge themselves on the overly self-confident Courbet for all his provocations and swaggering: he was—probably unjustly—held responsible for the pulling down of the Vendôme Column, a national symbol. The artist was not only imprisoned for a few months but also condemned to pay over 300,000 francs in yearly installments of 10,000 francs to have the monument rebuilt. He had just put together the money for the first payment at the time of his death.

In artistic terms as well, Courbet seems to have passed his zenith, although the Swiss landscape's effect on him was nothing less than amazing, inspiring him to paint panoramic Alpine views of which the importance has until now been underestimated.[87] Exhibitions of his works were organized in Switzerland, where they found numerous admirers, including the young Ferdinand Hodler (1853–1918).[88] His landscapes continued as before to sell well and were increasingly purchased by the bourgeoisie that served as the mainstay of the very state against which Courbet had fought—just one of the many contradictions in Courbet's life.[89] Courbet employed assistants to help him meet the demand for his work, but this was sometimes at the expense of quality. Even today, the question concerning studio participation in his paintings is an unsolved problem for the compilation of a new catalogue raisonné.

In 1877, it had been quite a while since he had made his mark in the art world and generated scandals with his realistic, large-format paintings. Numerous rumors were afloat concerning his *The Origin of the World* (ill. p. 94/95), but the public at large could not view the painting. Others had long since assumed the mantle of the avant-garde—first and foremost Edouard Manet, but also the Impressionists from the circle of Claude Monet, a friend of Courbet's. The revolution in painting technique set off by Courbet had been continued primarily by the Impressionists; the significance his handling of color was to have for the development of art up to and including Modernism would only be recognized much later.

What about Courbet's late idyllic landscapes: Are they not at variance with Realism, which was obliged to show the unvarnished truth? One example is the large-format painting dating from 1867 entitled *La bergère* or *La fileuse bretonne* (*The Shepherdess* or *Breton Spinner*, ill. p. 102/103), which hung for many years in the living area of the home of Albert C. Barnes in Merion, Pennsylvania, near Philadelphia.[90] We see a young peasant girl dressed in traditional garb spinning; she is sitting under a tree, accompanied by a black dog that is reminiscent of Courbet's dog in his 1844 self-portrait (cover illustration). The vast expanse of the sea is visible in the background. To the right is a meadow with grazing sheep seen against the backdrop of a stand of trees through which a farmhouse comes into view. The picture, which reads like a pasticcio of Courbet's motifs, was painted with great delicacy—again with liberal use of the palette knife—and shows wonderful variety in the gradations of color. But is it perhaps *too* beautiful? It is possible that some critique of existing conditions lurks beneath the surface of this exaggerated idyll? One should perhaps see Courbet's late landscapes fundamentally as counterparts to the images of contemporary life painted by Manet and the Impressionists.[91]

Idylls as counter-worlds, large-scale realistic paintings, pictures charged with sexual innuendo, and exceedingly innovative, revolutionary landscapes: these are undoubtedly Courbet's major historical achievements. When we look at his oeuvre in this way, the focus is primarily on his motifs. He was a key innovator in terms of *what* he painted. But it cannot be emphasized

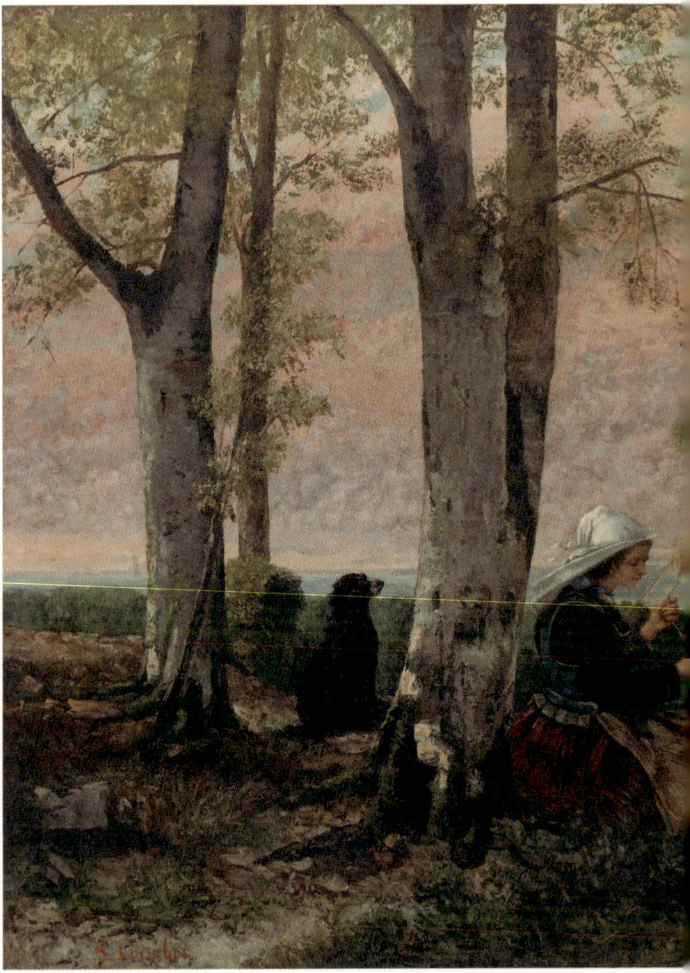

Gustave Courbet, *La bergère* or *La fileuse bretonne (The Shepherdess* or *Breton Spinner)*, 1867, oil on canvas, 128.9 × 199.4 cm, The Barnes Foundation, Philadelphia

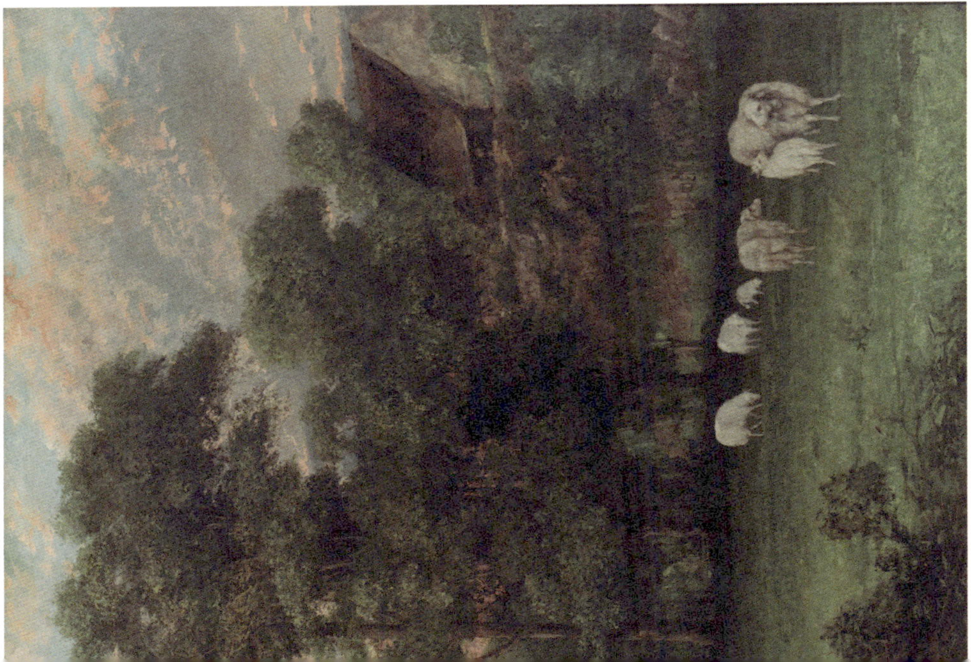

enough that *how* he painted was perhaps of even greater significance for the development of art. The painter Neo Rauch (b. 1960) once wrote in an essay about a picture of a wave that Courbet "let painting impose its will on him and the motif; he unlocked a small banqueting chamber for painting, which filled it with wild lust."[92] The extent to which painting is as arbitrary as Rauch suggests remains open. But surely painting in and of itself had never been granted as much space as Courbet granted it. This does not mean it was non-representational or abstract. In Courbet's work, painting appears—perhaps for the first time in the history of art—not only as a means of representation but also as a true artistic subject.

Notes

1 Franz Schubert, *The Complete Song Texts,* trans. Richard Wigmore (Gollancz, 1988).

2 For example, in Petra ten-Doesschate Chu's text on the painting in Mariantonia Reinhard-Felice, ed., *Oskar Reinhart Collection "Am Römerholz" Winterthur: Complete Catalogue* (Basel, 2006), pp. 403–05.

3 I am grateful to Hansjörg Küster and Ansgar Hoppe for pointing this out to me.

4 Britta-Juliane Kruse, *Verborgene Heilkünste: Geschichte der Frauenmedizin im Spätmittelalter,* Quellen und Forschungen zur Literatur- und Kulturgeschichte 5 (Berlin and New York, 1996), p. 171.

5 Cited from *Gustave Courbet*, exh. cat. The Metropolitan Museum of Art (New York, 2008), p. 293.

6 Bruno Mottin discusses this point in his essay on the *Three Bathers* in the catalogue to the Courbet exhibition at the Fondation Beyeler; see Ulf Küster, ed., *Gustave Courbet,* exh. cat. Fondation Beyeler, Riehen / Basel (Ostfildern, 2014), pp. 106–13.

7 See the compilation of the dates in Marie-Hélène Lavallée and Bérangère Galy, *Gustave Courbet, d'Ornans* (Gollion, 2007), p. 166.

8 See *Courbet en son terroire: Les carnets du Musée Gustave Courbet,* edited by Pascale Bonnet, available at http://www.doubs.fr/pays-de-courbet/v2/fichespedago/Carnet1_web.html, here p. 2.

9 Pascal Reilé, "Les parcours initiatiques de l'enfant d'Ornans," in Yves Sarfati, ed., *Transferts de Courbet* (Dijon, 2013), pp. 77–107, here p. 92*ff.*

10 *Courbet en son terroire* (see note 8).

11 Michèle Haddad, *Gustave Courbet: Peinture et histoire* (Sainte-Croix, 2007), esp. pp. 33–39. On *A Burial*: pp. 45–68.

12 On the system of genres, which is only touched on here, see Werner Busch, *Das sentimentalische Bild: Die Krise der Kunst im 18. Jahrhundert und die Geburt der Moderne* (Munich, 1993) pp. 22–24.

13 *Letters of Gustave Courbet,* ed. and trans. Petra ten-Doesschate Chu (Chicago, 1992), no. 45-3, p. 53.

14 The photograph is located in the photographic files of the National Gallery of Art, Washington DC. A recurring problem in the viewing of

Courbet's painting is that the varnish (i.e. the finish used to protect the picture's surface) has darkened. Removing the varnish—even for restoring the paintings—is extraordinarily difficult because there is always a danger of damaging the underlying layers of varnish, which Courbet applied in a highly differentiated fashion. Courbet's complicated and unconventional painting technique has not been thoroughly investigated. I am grateful for conversations with conservators Ann Hoenigswald (National Gallery of Art, Washington DC) and Markus Gross (Fondation Beyeler, Riehen / Basel).

15 This is suggested by a preliminary drawing in the Musée des Beaux-Arts et d'Archéologie in Besançon; see illustration in Laurence des Cars et al., eds., *Gustave Courbet,* exh. cat. Galeries Nationales du Grand Palais, Paris; The Metropolitan Museum of Art, New York; Musée Fabre, Montpellier (Paris, 2007), p. 175.

16 *Letters* (see note 13), no. 50-1, p. 91*ff.* For a who's who of the painting, see Jean-Luc Mayaud, *Courbet: L'Enterrement à Ornans: Un tombeau pour la République* (Paris, 1999), pp. 83–158.

17 Claudette R. Mainzer, "Who is Buried at Ornans?" *Courbet Reconsidered,* exh. cat. The Brooklyn Museum, New York; The Minneapolis Institute of Arts, Minneapolis (New York, 1988), pp. 77–81.

18 On David's influence, Paris 2007 (see note 15), pp. 174–81, with additional literature. Dutch group portraits, which likewise could have served as models for this painting, are also indicated here.

19 These two figures could have been modeled after the figures at the right in Benjamin West's stylistically influential history painting of 1770, *The Death of General Wolfe.*

20 In a speech at Antwerp; see Klaus Herding, ed., *Realismus als Widerspruch: Die Wirklichkeit in Courbets Malerei* (Frankfurt am Main, 1978), p. 28.

21 *Heine's Book of Songs,* trans. Charles G. Leland (New York, 1884) p. 69.

22 Letter to Champfleury, *Letters* (see note 13), no. 50-1, p. 91–92.

23 Herding 1978 (see note 20), p. 30. Cited from Fritz Novotny, *Painting and Sculpture in Europe 1780–1880* (New Haven and London, 1995), p. 249.

24 Compare the description of the painting in Jean-Luc Mayaud, *Les paysans du Doubs au temps de Courbet (Annales litteraires de l'université de Besançon)* (Paris, 1979), between p. 124 and 125.

25 Paris 2007 (see note 15), pp. 158–60.

26 The question is, of course, whether Courbet had access to the Amsterdam Town Hall. Quellinus's work has, however, been reproduced; see the illustration at http://library.artstor.org/.

27 See Daumier's *Pastorales,* a series of caricatures published in 1845.

28 T. J. Clark, "A Bourgeois Dance of Death: Max Buchon on Courbet," *Burlington Magazine* 111 (April–May 1969), pp. 208–12, 282–89.

29 Alexandre Schanne, *Souvenirs de Schaunard* (Paris, 1887), p. 301, cited from James Henry Rubin, *Realism and Social Vision in Courbet & Proudhon* (Princeton, 1980), p. xv.

30 Georges Riat, *Gustave Courbet,* trans. Michael Locey (New York, 2008), p. 39.

31 *Letters* (see note 13), no. 49-8, p. 88. The translation follows that of Michael Nungesser in "Die Steinklopfer," in Klaus Herding und Werner Hofmann, eds., *Courbet und Deutschland,* exh. cat. Hamburger Kunsthalle, Städtische Galerie im Städelschen Kunstinstitut, Frankfurt am Main (Cologne, 1978), pp. 560–73, here p. 560.

32 This is suggested by a remark made by Courbet in a letter from April 1840, in which he writes that his father now has "all the Flagey lands." See *Letters* (see note 13), no. 40-1, p. 32.

33 On the land reforms of the nineteenth century, see Hansjörg Küster, *Die Entdeckung der Landschaft: Einführung in eine neue Wissenschaft* (Munich, 2012), esp. p. 255.

34 *Letters* (see note 13), 50-1, p. 101.

35 Riat 2008 (see note 30), p. 39.

36 Compare Linda Nochlin, "The *Cribleuses de blé*: Courbet, Millet, Breton, Kollwitz and the Image of the Working Woman," *Courbet* (London, 2007), pp. 95–108, here p. 104 and note 38.

37 On the methods of winnowing grain, see Uwe Meiners, *Die Kornfege in Mitteleuropa: Wort- und sachkundliche Studien zur Geschichte einer frühen landwirtschaftlichen Maschine* (Münster, 1983), pp. 114–27. Sifting the grain is also possible but that does not seem to be depicted here (p. 138): the person at the left sits in the refuse, not in the grain—just as the figure in the middle does not kneel on the grain, which, because it is precious, is being gathered in a bowl. As such, Michael Fried's interpretation of the chaff that falls like pigment onto a canvas is incorrect, although his idea—referencing Jackson Pollock's dripping technique—is fascinating. See Michael Fried, *Courbet's Realism* (Chicago and London, 1992), p. 152*ff.*

38 Haddad 2007 (see note 11), pp. 127–31, esp. p. 128.

39 See http://dingler.culture.hu-berlin.de/article/pj103/ar103021 (accessed July 7, 2014).

40 *Letters* (see note 13), no. 48-3, pp. 78–79.

41 "Mais la disposition des jambes est plus que triviale; elle est presque indécente." Translated from Edmond About, *Voyage à travers l'exposition des beaux-arts (peinture et sculpture)* (Paris, 1855), p. 204.

42 See, for example, Werner Hofmann, "Courbets Wirklichkeiten," in

Hamburg / Frankfurt 1978 (see note 31), pp. 590–613, here p. 600.

43 Vincent Pomarède et al., eds., *Ingres 1780–1867*, exh. cat. Louvre (Paris, 2006), cat. 42. I am grateful to David Schmidhauser for pointing out that the motif of a woman looking into a chest frequently occurs in paintings of the School of Fontainebleau. Courbet could also have found his inspiration here. The *Venus of Urbino* was also a model for many of his other female nudes.

44 Eugène Delacroix, *Journal (1822–1857)*, ed. Michèle Hanoosh, vol. 1 (Paris, 2009), p. 929. This and subsequent quotations are cited from Stephen Eisenman, "The Rhetoric of Realism: Courbet and the Origins of the Avant-Garde," *Nineteenth-Century Art: A Critical History* (London, 2007), p. 221.

45 On Courbet as an "exhibition artist," see Oskar Bätschmann, *Ausstellungskünstler: Kult und Karriere im modernen Kunstsystem* (Cologne, 1997), pp. 124–33.

46 *Letters* (see note 13), no. 54-8, p. 133.

47 This extraordinarily important work in Courbet's oeuvre has been the subject of countless books and essays. Of course, dealing with them comprehensively would far exceed the scope of this chapter. The most recent extensive monograph on the painting is Werner Hofmann, *Das Atelier: Courbets Jahrhundertbild* (Munich, 2010).

48 Translated from Heinrich Heine, "Französische Maler: Gemäldeausstellung in Paris 1831," Werke, ed. Stuart Atkins, vol. 2, bk. 1, *Der Salon* (Munich, 1978), p. 24*ff.*

49 *Letters* (see note 13), no. 55-1, p. 135.

50 *Letters* (see note 13), no. 54-8, p. 133.

51 See note 44.

52 To employ an image devised by Michael Fried, in Fried 1992 (see note 37), p. 161.

53 The English translation is cited from Robert Goldwater and Marco Treves, eds., *Artists on Art from the XIV to XX Century*, 3rd ed. (New York, 1958), p. 295. The text was supposedly edited by Champfleury or Castagnary; see Herding 1978 (see note 20), p. 27. Many of the formulations greatly resemble those written by Courbet in a letter to his friend Alfred Bruyas in Montpellier (*Letters* [see note 13], no. 53-6, pp. 114–18); the possibility that Courbet was the sole author cannot therefore be excluded.

54 See Laurence des Cars in Paris 2007 (see note 15), pp. 91–93.

55 Letter to Alfred Bruyas, May 3, 1854; *Letters* (see note 13), 54-2, p. 122*ff.*

56 For the following, see the catalogue entry by Sylvain Amic in Paris 2007 (see note 15), pp. 104–06.

57 Idem., p. 104.

58 See the text by Bruno Mottin on the *Three Bathers* (ill. p. 15) in the catalogue of the 2014 Courbet exhibition at the Fondation Beyeler; these were also overpainted multiple times. See Riehen 2014 (see note 6), pp. 106–13.

59 Compare Sylvain Amic and Florence Hudowicz, "Courbet's 'Classical Walpurgis Night': A Vanished Work Resurfaces," in Klaus Herding and Max Hollein, eds., *Courbet: A Dream of Modern Art,* exh. cat. Shirn Kunsthalle, Frankfurt 2010/2011 (Ostfildern, 2010), pp. 43–51.

60 Ségolène Le Men, "Courbet: Déplacements et déguisements," in Yves Sarfati, ed., *Transferts de Courbet* (Dijon, 2013), pp. 109–34, esp. pp. 114–20. Raphael Rosenberg pointed out the handprint—which, however, is painted.

61 Anne M. Wagner, "Courbet's Landscapes and Their Market," in *Art History* 4 (December 1981), pp. 410–30.

62 See the brief section on the significance of the sketch in France by Werner Busch, *Die notwendige Arabeske: Wirklichkeitsaneignung und Stilisierung in der deutschen Kunst des 19. Jahrhunderts* (Berlin, 1985), pp. 257–61.

63 The most important publication on this subject is Paul Galvez, *Gustave Courbet and the Origins of Modern Painting 1862–1870,* Ph.D. diss. (Columbia University, 2008).

64 Translated from Schanne 1887 (see note 29), p. 288.

65 On Courbet's use of the palette knife, see Matthias Krüger, "Gespachtelter Zufall: Gustave Courbet und die Messermalerei," in Philippe Cordez and Matthias Krüger, eds., *Werkzeuge und Instrumente* (Berlin, 2012), pp. 109–27.

66 In conversation with the author, 2013.

67 Joachim Gasquet's *Cezanne: A Memoir With Conversations,* trans. Christopher Pemberton (London, 1991), p. 144.

68 A winter landscape with deer that has since been lost; see Robert Fernier, *La vie et l'œuvre de Gustave Courbet: Catalogue raisonné,* 2 vols. (Lausanne and Paris, 1977/78), F. 566.

69 Translated from Paul Meyerheim, "Adolph von Menzel: Erinnerungen," in Gisold Lammel, ed., *Exzellenz lassen bitten: Erinnerungen an Adolph Menzel* (Berlin, 1992), pp. 157–235, here p. 197.

70 Dietmar Elger, *Gerhard Richter: Catalogue raisonné,* vol. 3 (Ostfildern, 2013), nos. 615 and 616.

71 Guy de Maupassant, "La vie d'un paysagiste," September 28, 1886. An English translation of the relevant passage is cited in Mary Morton and Charlotte Eyerman, eds., *Courbet and the Modern Landscape,* exh. cat. J. Paul Getty Museum (Los Angeles, 2006), p. 104*ff.*

72 Illustrated, for example, in Paris 2007 (see note 15), p. 289.

73 I wish to thank Markus Gross, head conservator at the Fondation Beyeler, for this information.

74 Translated from Meyerheim 1992 (see note 69), pp. 197–99.

75 Gasquet 1991 (see note 67), p. 178.

76 Cited from Pierre Schneider, *Louvre Dialogues,* trans. Patricia Southgate (New York, 1971), p. 38.

77 Here Courbet places himself in a long tradition of depicting geological formations. However, we can only observe the congruence between what is represented and the material to be illustrated in his work; see Oskar Bätschmann, *Entfernung der Natur: Landschaftsmalerei 1750–1920* (Cologne, 1989), pp. 57–67, esp. p. 67.

78 The quotes from Courbet's conversation with Max Claudet are cited in Los Angeles 2006 (see note 71), p. 40.

79 Paris 2007 (see note 15), pp. 398 and 405.

80 Courbet's inscription "Dame Verte" ("Green Lady") on a drawing of a grotto (Musée d'Orsay, inv. RF 29234, 17) shows that he was familiar with this designation. "Dame verte" is the name given to several grottos in the French Jura, one of which is supposed to be near Ornans.

81 For additional literature, see http://juraspeleo.ffspeleo.fr/divers/legendes/legendes.htm (accessed July 18, 2014).

82 See also Isolde Pludermacher, "L'Origine du monde: Entre imaginaire scientifique et poétique," in Frédérique Thomas-Maurin, ed., *Cet obscur objet de desires: Autour de L'origine du monde,* exh. cat. Musée Courbet Ornans (Paris, 2014), pp. 115–30, here p. 118*ff.*

83 See the seminal work by Thierry Savatier, *L'origine du monde: Histoire d'un tableau de Gustave Courbet,* 4th ed. (Paris, 2009). See also the essay by Laurence Madeline in Küster 2014 (see note 5), pp. 138–47.

84 In the book *Trois dîners avec Gambetta,* edited by his son in 1929; cited from Linda Nochlin, "Courbet's 'L'origine du monde': The Origin without an Original," *October 37* (Summer 1986), pp. 76–86, here p. 80.

85 See the information on the website of the Museum Thyssen-Bornemisza in Madrid: http://www.museothyssen.org/en/thyssen/ficha_obra/455 (accessed July 7, 2014). Courbet must also have been able to draw on the photographs reproduced in Paris 2007 when he painted the picture (see note 15, p. 383ff). Unlike Courbet's work, however, these depict stimulated female genitals and are clearly pornographic.

86 Here I refer to the exhibition *Cet obscur objet de desires: Autour de l'origine du monde,* which opens in the summer of 2014 at the Musée Courbet. Only a few years after acquiring the painting, Khalil Bey had to sell his collection. The picture was long owned by the Hungarian Baron Ferenc Hatvany, later by the psychoanalyst Jacques Lacan and his wife Sylvie Bataille. Since 1995 it has been in the Musée d'Orsay in Paris. It was

exhibited for the first time outside France in 2008 in conjunction with the Courbet retrospective at the Metropolitan Museum in New York. In 2014, the painting will be on show for the first time in Europe outside France in the Courbet exhibition at the Fondation Beyeler, Riehen / Basel.

87 The Musée d'art et d'histoire in Geneva is devoting an exhibition to Courbet's time in Switzerland, which will open in the fall of 2014; Laurence Madeline, ed., *Courbet: Les années suisses,* exh. cat. Musée d'art et d'histoire (Geneva, 2014).

88 Ulf Küster, *Ferdinand Hodler* (Ostfildern, 2012), p. 43*ff.*

89 Oskar Bätschmann, "The Artist on Show: Gustave Courbet," *Representation and Show,* Shida Studies in Art History 2 (Taipei, 2013), pp. 1–39, esp. p. 24*ff.*

90 The painting will be probably on view for the very first time in conjunction with the comprehensive Courbet exhibition at the Fondation Beyeler in Riehen / Basel in 2014.

91 As argued by Galvez 2008.

92 Translated from Neo Rauch, "Meeresungeheuer und Schaumgeburten," in Felix Krämer and Max Hollein, eds., *Kunst der Moderne 1800–1945 im Städel Museum* (Ostfildern, 2011), p. 28*ff.*

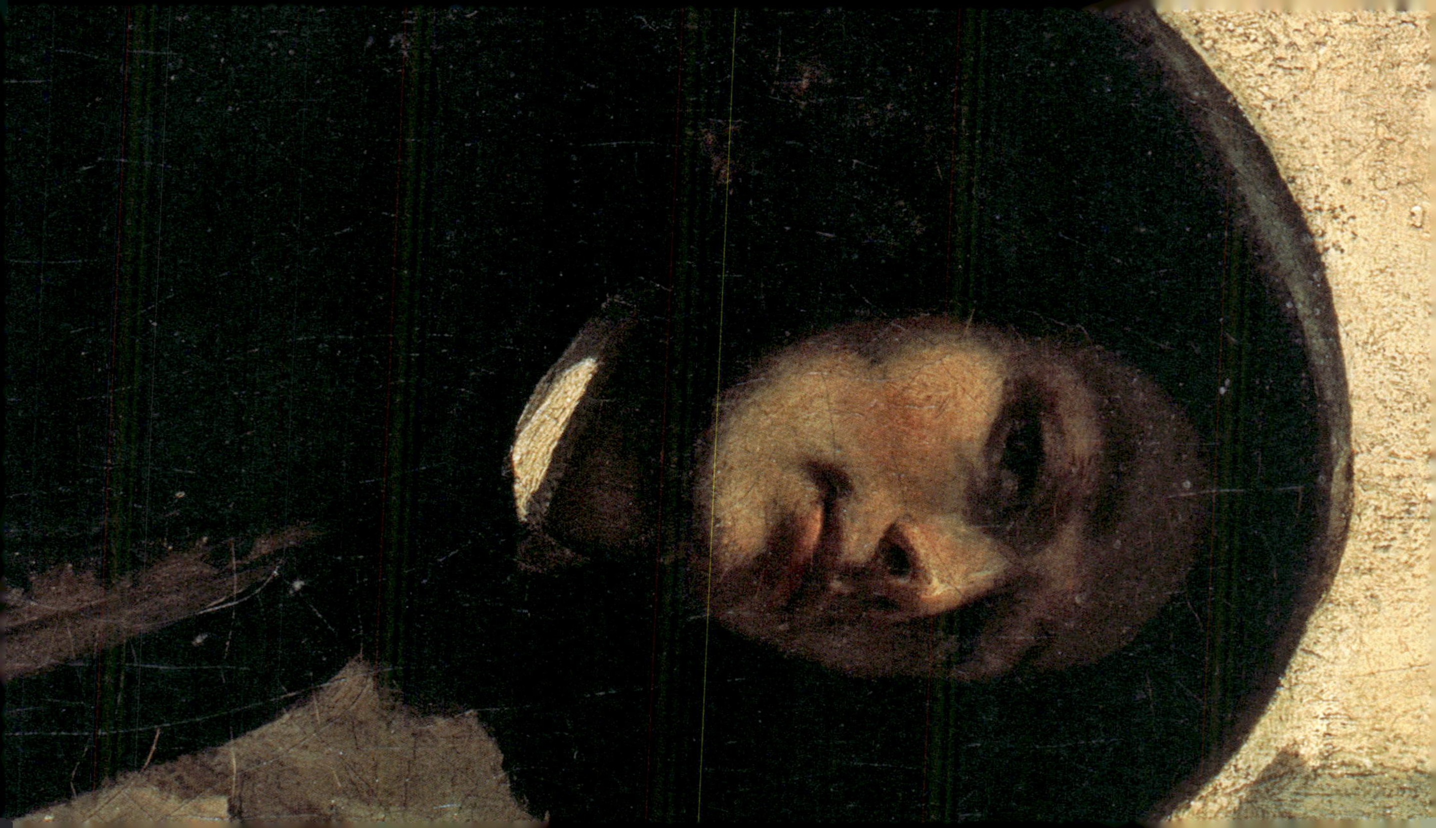

Biography

1819

Jean Désiré Gustave Courbet is born on June 10 in or near Ornans (see p. 17*ff*). His father, Régis Courbet, is a prosperous landholder and owns a farm in the nearby village of Flagey. His mother, Suzanne Silvie, née Oudot, comes from a long-established Ornans family. Gustave has four younger sisters.

1831–1837

Attends school at Ornans. First drawing lessons in 1833.

1837–1839

Attends the Collège Royale in Besançon. Takes drawing lessons from Charles-Antoine Flajoulot, a pupil of Jacques-Louis David.

1839

Moves to Paris. Interrupted only by travels and longer sojourns, especially in Ornans, Courbet lives there until 1874. Trains as a painter in the studios of Carl August von Steuben and Nicolas-Auguste Hesse, but is for the most part an autodidact. He receives financial support from his family.

1844
The *Portrait of the Artist,* known as *Courbet with a Black Dog* (cover illustration), is the first painting Courbet is able to exhibit at the Salon.

1846/47
Travels to Belgium and the Netherlands.

1847
Befriends the writer and anarchist Pierre-Joseph Proudhon and Charles Baudelaire. Courbet's son Désiré Alfred Emile is born out of wedlock on September 15. The mother, Virginie Binet, poses regularly for the artist; with her son, she leaves him in 1851.

1848
A declared pacifist, Courbet does not take part in the revolution. He is one of the Bohemian artists who frequents the Brasserie Andler.

1849
Courbet is awarded a gold medal for his painting *Une après-dînée à Ornans (An After Dinner at Ornans),* which is on show at the Salon. As a result, he no longer requires approval from the Salon's jury to show his works there.

1850
Courbet exhibits his so-called "Realism Trilogy" comprising *A Burial at Ornans* (ill. p. 22/23), *The Stonebreakers* (ill. p. 36) and *The Peasants of Flagey Returning from the Fair, Ornans* (ill. p. 30/31) at the Salon.

1853
Alfred Bruyas from Montpellier becomes Courbet's most important patron and collector.

1854
Courbet lives with Alfred Bruyas in Montpellier from late May to September. He paints *Bonjour Monsieur Courbet (Good Day, Monsieur Courbet)* and *Le bord de mer à Palavas (The Beach at Palavas).*

1855
In addition to his eleven paintings on show at the Paris Exposition Universelle, Courbet exhibits forty more of his works in a purpose-built pavilion he names "Realism." These include his monumental programmatic painting *The Artist's Studio* (ill. p. 54/55).

1858
After trips to Germany in 1851 and 1856, where he has many admirers, Courbet sojourns in Frankfurt am Main.

1862
Courbet spends a year with Etienne Baudry in the Saintonge region north of Bordeaux, where he chiefly paints flower still lifes and landscapes.

1864
Paints numerous landscapes at Ornans, including a series depicting the source of the Loue River.

1865
Death of his friend Pierre-Joseph Proudhon. Visits Trouville, where he meets Claude Monet, James Abbott McNeill Whistler, and Joanna Hiffernan. Courbet paints numerous seascapes.

1866
Travels to the seaside at Deauville with Eugène Boudin and Claude Monet. Paints *Le sommeil (Sleep)* and *The Origin of the World* (ill. p. 94/95) for Khalil Bey.

1867
Courbet again organizes his own separate exhibition parallel to the International Exposition and shows over 100 works.

1869

Visits Étretat: paints seascapes and views of the coast. He is given a gallery of his own at the International Art Exhibition in Munich. King Ludwig II of Bavaria awards him the Knight's Cross, First Class, from the Order of St. Michael.

1870

Courbet rejects membership in the French Legion of Honor. After the abdication of Napoleon III he is elected president of the Arts Commission and the archive on September 6. On September 18 Courbet suggests that the Vendôme Column celebrating the Napoleonic Wars be dismantled.

1871

Courbet is elected a deputy of Paris Commune and a delegate of the Arts Commission in April. The Communards demolish the Vendôme Column on May 16. Courbet is arrested shortly after the suppression of the Commune; he is sentenced to six months in prison and fined.

1872

On May 1 returns to his studio, which has been plundered. Stays in Ornans with his assistants Cherubino Pata and Marcel Ordinaire.

1873

After the National Assembly decides to rebuild the Vendôme Column, the confiscation of Courbet's possessions is ordered. Courbet flees to Switzerland on July 23, settling in La Tour-de-Peilz on Lake Geneva in October. He buys an old boarding house, where his assistants also live.

1874

Courbet is made solely responsible for the destruction of the Vendôme Column and sentenced to pay all costs for its reconstruction—over 300,000 francs.

1877

Courbet's health takes a turn for the worse at year's end and he dies in exile in Switzerland at La Tour-de-Peilz on December 31.

Recommended Reading and Viewing

For those interested in learning more about Courbet, we heartily recommend visiting the exhibitions to be shown in parallel at the Fondation Beyeler in Riehen / Basel and the Musée d'art et d'histoire in Geneva in 2014/15, each of which will be accompanied by catalogues. Courbet's large, monumental paintings (and many of his other works) can be found at the Musée d'Orsay in Paris. Other important collections of his paintings are in the Metropolitan Museum of Art, New York, and the Musée Fabre, Montpellier. The Musée Courbet in Ornans regularly organizes interesting exhibitions and congresses on the artist and is well suited as a starting point for excursions to the sites associated with Courbet's life and work in the Franche-Comté.

Literature

Though the vast Courbet bibliography is highly diverse, three recent exhibition catalogues provide an overview of the current state of Courbet research and can serve as the starting point for further reading and viewing:

Courbet: A Dream of Modern Art, edited by Klaus Herding and Max Hollein, exh. cat. Schirn Kunsthalle Frankfurt am Main (Ostfildern, 2010).

Gustave Courbet, edited by Laurence des Cars et al., exh. cat. Réunion des musées nationaux – Grand Palais, Paris; Metropolitan Museum of Art, New York; Musée Fabre, Montpellier (New York, 2008).

Courbet and the Modern Landscape, edited by Mary Morton and Charlotte Eyerman, exh. cat. J. Paul Getty Museum, Los Angeles; Museum of Fine Arts, Houston; Walters Art Museum, Baltimore (Los Angeles, 2006).

Acknowledgments

Large portions of this book were written while I was an Ailsa Mellon Bruce Visiting Senior Fellow at the Center for Advanced Study in the Visual Arts (CASVA) at the National Gallery of Art in Washington DC. I am grateful to Dean Elizabeth Cropper, Associate Dean Therese O'Malley, and Associate Dean Peter Lukehart for their kind support.

For advice and suggestions I furthermore wish to extend my gratitude to Simone Albiez, Oskar Bätschmann, Andreas Beyer, Barbara Buckley, S. Hollis Clayson, Peter Doig, Sarah Faunce, Markus Gross, Stéphane Guégan, Klaus Herding, Ann Hoenigswald, Ansgar Hoppe, Jason Kaufman, Sam Keller, Hansjörg Küster, David Lubin, Laurence Madeline, Mary Morton, Lorenzo Pericolo, Noëlle Pia, Andreas Platzgummer, Isolde Pludermacher, Neo Rauch, Jan Rothschild, James H. Rubin, David Schmidhauser, Cristina Steingräber, and Frédérique Thomas-Maurin.

Remembering the glow of the evening sun at the Capitol, I dedicate this book to Annina und Leonard.

Gustave Courbet

Ulf Küster

Translation Michael Wolfson

Copyediting Irene Schaudies

Graphic design and typesetting Andreas Platzgummer, Hatje Cantz

Typeface Adobe Caslon Pro, News Gothic MT Std

Production Christine Stricker, Hatje Cantz

Reproductions LVD Gesellschaft für Datenverarbeitung mbH, Berlin

Paper Fly 05 hochweiß, 100 g/m^2

Printing Offizin Scheufele, Stuttgart

Binding Nädele, Verlags- und Industriebuchbinderei, Nehren

Photo credits

The Barnes Foundation, Philadelphia: pp. 102/103; bpk / RMN – Grand Palais / Hervé Lewandowski: pp. 94/95; bpk / RMN – Grand Palais / Jacques L'Hoir / Jean Popovitch: cover, p. 114; bpk / RMN – Grand Palais / Patrice Schmidt: p. 91; bpk / The Metropolitan Museum of Art, New York: p. 90; bpk / Staatliche Kunstsammlungen Dresden: p. 36; Brooklyn Museum, 41.1256: pp. 74, 77; Eric Emo / Petit Palais / Roger-Viollet: p. 15; Galleria Nazionale d'Arte Moderna, Rome, by permission of Ministero per I Beni e le Attività Culturali / Antonio Idini: pp. 86/87; Museo Thyssen-Bornemisza, Madrid: p. 97; The National Museum for Art, Architecture, and Design, Oslo / Anne Hansteen Jarre: pp. 2, 69; NGA Images, National Gallery of Art, Washington DC: pp. 82/83; Private collection: p. 80; RMN – Grand Palais (Musée d'Orsay) / Agence Bulloz: pp. 30/31; RMN – Grand Palais (Musée d'Orsay) / Gérard Blot / Hervé Lewandowski: pp. 22/23, 54/55, 60/61, 65; RMN – Photograph: Gérard Blot: pp. 44/45; Sammlung Oskar Reinhart "Am Römerholz," Winterthur: pp. 10/11, 14; The Walters Art Museum, Baltimore: p. 46

Published by Hatje Cantz Verlag
Zeppelinstrasse 32
73760 Ostfildern
Germany
Tel. +49 711 4405-200
Fax +49 711 4405-220
www.hatjecantz.de
A Ganske Publishing Group company

Hatje Cantz books are available internationally at selected bookstores. For more information about our distribution partners, please visit our website at www.hatjecantz.com.

ISBN 978-3-7757-3877-4 (English)
ISBN 978-3-7757-3861-3 (German)

Also available as e-book
ISBN 978-3-7757-3878-1 (English)
ISBN 978-3-7757-3867-5 (German)

Printed in Germany

Cover illustration
Gustave Courbet, *Portrait de l'artiste,* known as *Courbet au chien noir* (*Portrait of the Artist,* known as *Courbet with a Black Dog*), ca. 1843, 46.5 × 55.5 cm, Petit Palais, Musée des Beaux-Arts de la Ville de Paris

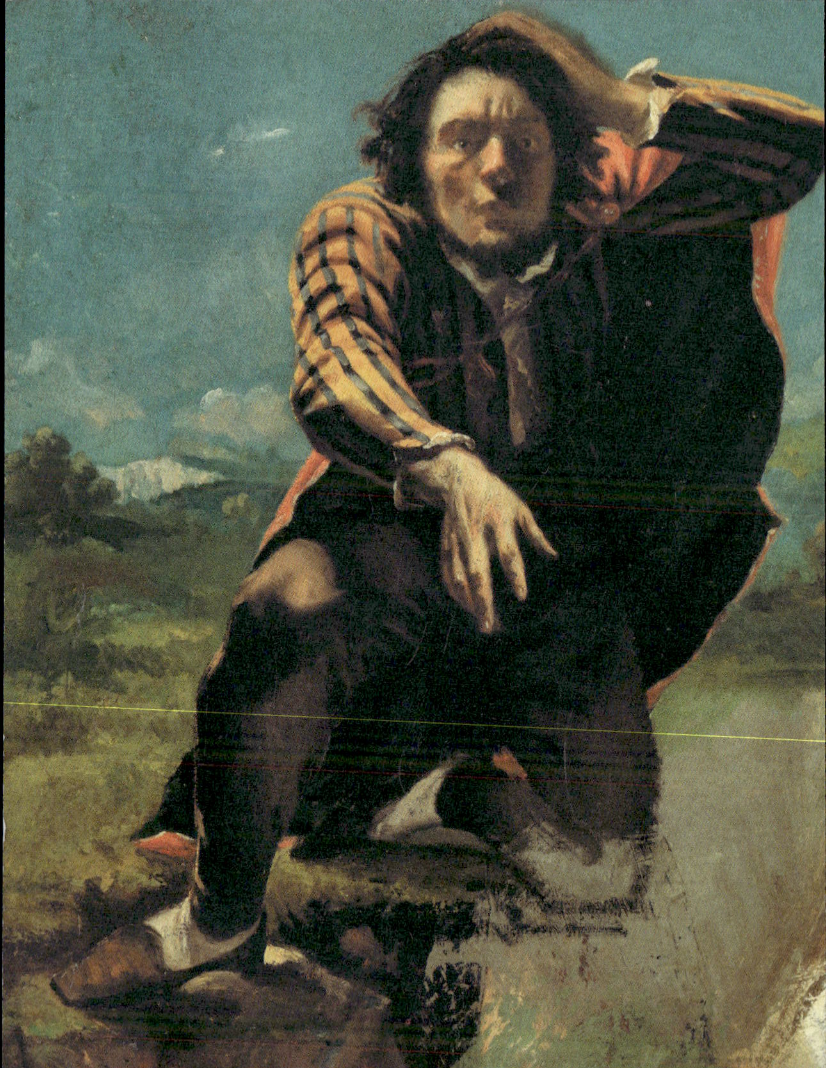